Widowhood, I Didn't Ask For This

E L A I N E   M A R Z E

ISBN 978-1-68570-240-3 (paperback)
ISBN 978-1-68570-241-0 (digital)

Christian Faith Publishing
832 Park Avenue
Meadville, PA 16335
www.christianfaithpublishing.com

Printed in the United States of America

To my mother, Mellionee Flores; my mother-in-law, Inez Marze; my sister, Linda Jeffries; women who walked this path before me; and so many friends. I can't list them all.

Contents

Foreword

Elaine Marze gets right to the heart of the matter when writing about widowhood. My husband of over forty years died suddenly, leaving me to face the rest of my life alone. It's not easy, but Elaine's perspective helped me to appreciate all the time we did have together. I'm left with a certain peace, knowing that Jimmie was a wonderful dad, husband, provider, and a friend to everyone. I could not have asked for more.

Edna Wheless, Editor/Publisher, *DeSoto Life* Magazine, Grand Cane, LA

I, too, have lost a husband at the age of fifty-seven. My loss was a sudden loss. Some have asked if I would rather it have been over time with an illness other than a sudden loss. To me, I believe one is just as bad as the other. In the end, the pain, the hurt, the loneliness, the grieving, the loss is still the same.

This book was given to me by a pastor friend who was trying to find some way to bring me comfort. I was desperately searching for something to fix my situation, so I read the entire book the night he gave it to me. Did it fix my broken life? *No!* But what it did do was bring me comfort in knowing that what I felt was normal and I wasn't the only *one* who has ever gone through this feeling, completely helpless and lost. I was normal! This is a book of hope; and with that, it brings peace and comfort in knowing you can make it to the other side—one day at a time!

Monica Moore

Introduction

I am officially a widow. I lost my husband five months ago (at the time of this writing). Luther Marze Jr. was my hero, my love, and my knight who came into my life not wearing shining armor but a navy uniform; and instead of riding a white horse, he was driving a 1968 yellow Dodge Super Bee with a four-speed manual stick shift. I was a young eighteen-year-old college student when we met on a blind date while he was on leave from the navy, and he had just returned from his second tour in Vietnam. We married a year later with my family celebrating the nuptials. He said that the first night we met, he knew I was "the one." I liked him too but was slower to evolve romantically than he was. However, it turned out that we had a marriage that inspired friends and family to say they wanted to have a love like ours, which was pretty high praise coming from those who know us well.

For nearly forty years, I tried to be the best wife possible. We saw eye to eye on politics, religion, and raising our family. My husband and I worked in our church, raised our kids according to the Holy Scriptures, and did our best not to commit immoral, ungodly, or illegal acts. I guess I thought there was an unwritten law somewhere that said there should be a reward for living and loving right.

Instead, I'm looking for someone (another widow or widower) to assure me that this pain will fade; but mostly, I have people doling out advice that I should move on with my life as though the last forty years never happened. Yes, I know; *life is for the living*. And I know that their intentions are good, but people need to understand that what I'm feeling deep inside is going to take time for me to deal with it. The abiding love of a long marriage carries with it too many memories to discard quickly or lightly.

Scripturally speaking, a chicken's pulley bone comes to mind where the Bible says a married couple should cleave together. Wouldn't a man and woman who have truly *cleaved* have to be forcefully and painfully broken apart to be separated? A single broken bone can be extremely painful as I learned from having broken an arm and leg, so how much more the tearing apart of heart, body, and mind when a beloved spouse dies?

Junior and I had a lot of adventures together mostly because he talked me into doing things I wouldn't have done otherwise. The man had no concept of fear. There's a good reason why, on reality television shows, it is nearly always males who try to skateboard down stair railings or ride a flying Jet Ski onto a crowded beach. Maybe it is a conqueror's mentality or just an overload of testosterone or, perhaps, a born-to-be-stupid genetic; but the male species have some really outlandish ideas about what they are capable of living through. It is for this reason that we women have so many opportunities to be thankful that our men survive all their "fun."

My own sweet husband had some very bad ideas of what constitutes good times, especially those plans that involved me directly. One time, he talked me into standing on a boat dock with water skis on my feet while he throttled the boat, supposedly to smoothly jerk me off the dock in a flying start to set me gently on the water's surface. What actually happened was a near fatality—mine! He said the tangled arms, legs, skis, and ropes that hit the water forty feet from the boat dock was my fault because I didn't keep my arms and legs gracefully parallel while in midair flight. My opinion, given loudly and excitedly much later when I could breathe again, was that when he realized my airborne body was traveling at superspeed with ski rope tangled around my right leg and left arm, one ski wrapped around my neck, and all of me tied to the speeding boat, he should have stopped a lot sooner—a whole lot sooner! His excuse that he looked for me in the sky before he searched the water didn't mollify me a bit. He said I should be thankful he towed me in before I drowned since I was too tangled up to save myself!

Then there was the time we went white-water rafting in *early* May in Colorado when our kids were seven and eight years old. Louisiana born and raised, we never considered that "winter runoff" (ice) would be so prevalent in May! Not only did we nearly freeze to death, but it was supposed to be an eight-hour float trip, and the water was so high and rough, and we were going so fast we did it in two hours.

Ten minutes after takeoff, we were too cold to scream. We were drenched by icy river water because we were under the water as much as we were above it; and we were moving so fast, the windchill factor probably equaled that of the Arctic Circle. Of course, our hot Louisiana weather heritage influenced our decision to wear shorts and tank tops for a day on the river. Who'd ever have dreamed our chill bumps could have chill bumps with little icicles hanging off them in May?

We were using all body parts, trying to stay in the raft; and I'm not too proud to share that I finally found a good use for my wide posterior cheeks because I'm not exaggerating when I say it wasn't only my hands that left clench marks on that raft! After finally reaching land again, we had to pry daughter Phaedra's fingers out of the rubber raft after we all scraped the ice off our eyelashes, enough for us to see.

I gave thanks to God that we survived with both our children intact, disregarding the frostbite and traumatic stress of bouncing off gigantic boulders in a rubber boat about the size of a bathtub while spending much of the time trying to hold our breath under unrelenting, rushing waves of ice water.

Our thirty-nine-plus years together were an adventure that ended October 19, 2011. It's going to take some getting used to.

Chapter 1

CURRENT STATUS

My daddy was killed when I was seven, so I grew up without knowing an earthly father's love and protection. Maybe I believed I was owed a lifelong husband. I admit to feeling a sense of betrayal toward God after my husband's death because He joined me in marriage to a man I not only loved, but I liked and respected. When my husband died, so did all our hopes, dreams, and plans. We truly did become one when we married. We had the cleaving part down to a fine art. But now, I feel like I lost half of myself—probably because I did.

Already, you can probably tell that this is not going to be a sweetly sentimental kind of book that tells you life on this side of marriage is going to be better and easier. Even before the funeral was over, people were giving me books and advice on grieving—books that either told me to "lean into my grief" or were full of psychobabble about the processes of grief. I decided there needed to be a book written fresh from the funeral, somebody who is keeping it real.

For the first two months after he died, Phaedra and I pretended that her daddy was away on a hunting trip in Colorado, and he would be coming home soon. Silly? Maybe. But we wanted to put off the reality of grieving as long as possible. And though it isn't working now that so much time has passed, it sure helped us get through the first weeks.

Over and over, I have been advised to grieve. People keep telling me I need to cry and scream and let it all out. But grieving means hurting, and I don't want to hurt any more than need be. I'm tired of hurting, knowing that my beloved husband is *gone forever*. By pretending that my man was going to be walking in the door at any time, I was delaying the hurt, and I'm thankful my brain went along with my desire to put off, as long as possible, that kind of emotional pain. The professionals call it denial. Well, let's hear it for denial! Naturally, I couldn't actually block out his death completely; but it gave me moments of respite, an emotional escape. Once I accepted that Luther Marze Jr. was gone, then I had to accept that I was alone in a way I hadn't been since I was nineteen years old. Most of my life was spent married to this man whom I adored, and I didn't know how to be without him. I didn't want to be without him. I didn't want to think of a future without him.

His role as husband was so essential to my life that no amount of imagining could comprehend a life without him. He embraced the role of lover, protector, helpmate, provider, best friend, and companion so completely and wholeheartedly that the hole he left was totally terrifying to me to try to comprehend.

When I explained how avoidance of his death helped delay the grieving process slightly, some helpful individual would tell me it wasn't healthy to put it (grieving) off—again, with the "you need to grieve" advice. That word *grieve* to me is a nice way of saying "a heart-wrenching hurt so deep my soul is screaming." But nobody hears, nor can they help if they did hear.

Why would it be wrong to put off some of the pain for as long as possible? In fact, I think it may be a self-healing kind of thing where our brains know we can't take any more emotional trauma at the time, so it goes along with the desire to live in denial for a while until we are ready to deal with the present reality. Of course, I'm no psychologist, but I am a widow. So though I can't speak to the official mental health side of the issue, I sure enough can speak to the widow part of it. Having said that, people who claim to be experts believe that not facing the existence of the loss is unhealthy, so suit yourself.

Something else I noticed then and since because more of my friends have become widows since Junior died, it seems that a whole lot of widows are taking anxiety drugs to get them through the dying and funeral and in the weeks afterward. I didn't have a prescription for tranquility pills. So I'm thinking now that if I had been taking some of those drugs, maybe I wouldn't have felt the need to pretend. Apparently, narcotics can pretend for you, so that should probably be a consideration too. Other widows under the influence of drugs say they have no memory of the funeral or weeks afterward—that it is just a hazy recollection. Their anguish didn't really begin until they came out from under the numbing benefit of pharmaceuticals, if they ever do.

People say that faith will fill the void; and certainly, Christ is a light that stands out in the darkness of such a loss. But being a Christian does not mean that we will not feel pain or that we will not miss a loved one. My Savior carried me through, but He didn't take away the hurting. In this life, there is gladness, and there is sorrow. Our Creator could have made roses without thorns, but He didn't. Life also has thorns—sharp, stabbing, cruel thorns that can draw blood. Yet some Christians who mean well will give grieving advice, like we will be exempt from anguish if we only have faith—not so.

Everybody quotes the stages of grief: denial, anger, bargaining with God, depression, and then the final acceptance of death/ loss. But those are just terms to those of us actually going through the process.

The two-and-a-half years of cancer treatments, surgeries, and wait-to-see-what-the-scans-showed episodes were stress filled, and most people probably thought I had prepared for widowhood. They would have been wrong. I thought it went against my Christian faith to prepare for the very thing we were praying *not* to happen, and I knew I could not function as well as I did if I let myself contemplate the predeath of my husband. Becoming a widow was an unpleasant surprise for me. Yes, I knew other people had survived a spouse's death, including my mother and mother-in-law; but until you experience it yourself, there are too many aspects you have (happily) been ignorant of previously.

Because Junior was told he was dying by all his doctors, we did prearrange our caskets and cemetery spots just in case they were right. Since that kind of planning can suck the joy right out of the day if we had let it, we cracked jokes the whole time we were choosing our final resting places and containers. I wasn't about to go to the funeral home and only make plans for his death. It just seemed insensitive. That's why I told him we'd go ahead and make death plans for both of us, especially since I figured that if he did die, I'd be right behind him with a stroke. I felt bad about the kids losing both parents at the same time, but I knew my place was at his side even if it was six feet below ground.

Actually, this was not the first time we planned for death. Mine. After my husband retired from the fire department, we went to Colorado in a fifth-wheel camper and were caught in the biggest snowstorm in one hundred years according to news reports. We were over 10,000 ft. elevation, about 350 feet below the top of a mountain where my husband had bought land and began building a log cabin. We had no cell phone service, and the snow was too deep to drive or walk out of it; and I inconveniently got altitude sickness, which escalated into cerebral and pulmonary edema. Everything in the camper froze, including us. I figured the least we could hope for was frostbite. Each day Junior climbed the 350 feet to the cabin site on top of the mountain to the recently installed (thank God) propane tank. We were there for six days with nobody in sight before a snowplow finally dug us out. And during that time, I should have died from either the cerebral or pulmonary edema. I was delirious most of the time. But during a cognitive period, we made plans on what Junior was to do with my body because, surely, I was dying (there but for the grace of God). Junior said he would keep my body in the camper, maybe lay me out on the couch. But I thought he ought to roll me out the door into the snow rather than keep a dead body inside the RV even if it was my body.

I made it to the hospital on the sixth day, and they told me I should be dead but sent me on oxygen to a lower altitude immediately; and it took weeks back in Louisiana to recover.

Normally, very much a realist, I was the last person to comprehend that my husband was dying, which is amazing to me even now. That denial stuff is real! I took Junior in to hospice on the advice of a hospice nurse who came to our home in the Ozarks to bring him morphine. The moment she walked in and looked at him, she rushed me to get him into hospice in an emergency run ninety minutes away. His throat cancer had spread, and big tumors were growing out of his chest, throat, and face; but I still thought he would rise up from the bed and say, "Come on, baby, let's go home." Since that time, I've talked with other widows who tell me they were the same way. In the grief books, that is called "denial." But between widows, it is called "hope." We didn't give up hope until there was absolutely no hope left.

One of my best friends came to hospice before my husband died, and she asked me, "Elaine, have you told Luther it is okay for him to go be with the Lord?" She told me later that I gave her a very ugly look and emphatically told her, "No, I haven't told him it is okay 'cause it's not okay! I want him to stay with me."

Marriage was and is God's plan for establishing the bedrock of society and giving us the emotional and physical closeness we need as couples to make it through the trials and tribulations of raising a family and growing old together. When that God-ordained unity is dissolved through no fault of a deeply committed couple, there is a tsunami of feelings and issues involved and unresolved.

As Christians, we know that we should "count it all joy," but the spiritual goal, our present hurt, and time of trouble must be suffered through as each of us is able. Well-meaning friends and relatives would do well to offer expressions of love without too much advice—unless they have actually walked this path.

Yes, Paul was in prison when he wrote about how the God of peace would be with us, and maybe it helps some people to be admonished to think positive; but the truth is that some of us haven't attained that level of spirituality yet. I've not lacked faith in God, but

I lacked the ability to be joyful as some kept telling me I should. That aspect of my faith has obviously not matured to the level where I can "count it all joy," particularly not the death of my husband.

One thing I have learned is that when you have lost your life's companion, it is easy to fear the future. I realized early on that it is very important *not* to worry about tomorrow, which is the same philosophy my husband and I tried to live by during the cancer. I wouldn't allow myself to cry (mostly) during cancer because when we were told that his cancer was terminal, he said he could handle "it" if I did not cry. He said it would break his heart to see me upset and crying, so he asked to please not cry. I knew that if the worse happened (and it did) that I'd have the rest of my life to cry. We didn't want to waste time we had together crying for what the future might bring. I've always known what God's Word says about worrying—basically, not to worry because God is in control. And I've tried to live by that. And certainly, during Junior's cancer, the prayers and help of the Holy Spirit gave us the peace we needed to not worry so much that we lost our joy and hope. Also, Junior was so strong, and he never faltered in his faith that our God is sufficient to carry us through any trouble that he inspired me too. Not to say that I didn't worry, but neither of us sat around crying or depressed. (I did lie on his chest at night and have some breakdowns; but for the most part, we just determined to count our blessings every day, hour, and minute.)

Before and since Junior's death, other people going through similar experiences (and there are a lot of them) asked me how we could handle the dying so well. One way was not to look ahead but just live in the here and now, minute by minute. There are many things, like finances and living arrangements, that have to be considered, but I quickly learned that if I thought about a holiday without Junior or eight years from now when granddaughter Kinsley graduates from high school without her papa there to see it, it would depress and scare me; so I knew I had to get my mind on something else. I am determined not to go there ahead of time if at all possible.

During Junior's sickness and my widowing, we have been blessed to have a lot of visitors, and that helps keep my mind off places it doesn't need to go. Also, I was able to keep working because as a writer (newsletters, ads, articles) for various companies, I am able to work from my computer at home or wherever. If there weren't any relatives, friends, or work around to keep my mind off the future, I'd start singing "O Happy Day" or "How Great Thou Art," whatever it took to establish mind control because I absolutely did not want to waste time being depressed or sad until I absolutely had to.

In the same vein, from talking to other widows and from my own experience, I know that if we carry tomorrow's burdens today, it can be unbearable. To contemplate all the meals for one; nights, holidays, and parties attended alone; making decisions with no help; the absence of physical love; etc. is to make oneself miserable. I am trying to discipline myself to live within the boundaries of today and, of course, to keep my sight and mind on the One who is in control and has the plan.

Chapter 2

What Not to Say

It was soon apparent that those people who were saying things like "Just lean on Jesus," and "You won't be lonely because our heavenly Father is going to wrap His big arms around you and hold you close" were people who had never lost their spouse. From other widows and widowers, I got: "It's hard. The hurt, the void will never go away. But with time and God's help, the pain eases some."

Straight out, let me say that without the grace and peace from God Almighty, I would never have made it through my husband's cancer and death. About that, there is no doubt! But there is a reason that marriage was ordained by God, and after decades together with the one you trust to have your back and hold your hand, you are going to miss him fiercely. The two of us had our own ways of communicating and could pretty much read each other's minds and finish each other's sentences. That person's death is going to wreak havoc with your formerly happy life.

Another platitude that widows hate is, "Toughen up! You need to move on."

Excuse me? We are living in the here and now. If we could jump ahead to the no-pain time, we probably would. But it is the present we are trying to get through, so don't dismiss it so easily. Comments like these are why some people shut themselves off from friends and relatives, which can lead to major depression and hopelessness. The more a widow or widower believes nobody understands his / her pain and feels absolutely alone, the more abandoned and despondent they feel. I say this a lot; but bottom line is, friends should talk less and listen more. Talking about the loss helps to work through the grief.

A particularly insensitive and obnoxious bit of counseling I received from two different people was that God might have taken my husband because I loved him too much or depended on him too much. Apparently, they meant that God was jealous because He thought I loved my husband more than I did Him. Please, folks, even if this is what you think, don't tell a grieving widow or widower that. The scriptures say that a husband is to love his wife as Christ loved the church and gave himself for it. He is told to love his wife more than his own body. As far as I can tell, there are no restrictions on loving a spouse; but though I know this, others might not, and such a statement could crush any spiritual comfort they might hope for.

Another sentiment that doesn't need to be shared is, "You took care of Junior when he had cancer, but what if you get sick? You won't have anybody to take care of you and be there for you like you were for him." Gee, thanks, I hadn't thought of that. There's enough fear of the future without having that idea thrown in my face.

Talked to a widow this week who said a friend told her, "I may not understand exactly how you feel, but my cat died last year so I can relate." Really! One of the worst comments I heard was at my husband's visitation: "Well, at least you'll only have half the dirty dishes and clothes to wash." Remember when Jesus cleaned out the temple with a whip? That's what I wanted to do to this woman.

I understand that people don't know what to say, and so they make regrettable statements. I am sure I have done the same thing. And some people are trying to show tough love and force us to move forward. But if they want to show sympathy and compassion, it is best not to voice these kinds of words of advice. Everybody moves and grieves at their own pace; it is not a forcible issue. Condemnation

9

and guilt might cause them to hide their feelings and go to an emotional underground where it is lonelier than ever and unhealthy too.

I am so blessed to have friends who did not get angry at me (or if they did, they hid it well) when I told them to hush with the advice until they were walking in my shoes. A few weeks after my husband died, another cancer patient's widow told me she decided to do what I did and be honest with some of her friends and relatives. She told them she didn't want any more advice; she just wanted them to listen to her heartache. It works. People who love you want to say and do what helps you, not what hurts you. But you may have to tell them straight out what you want to hear and what you don't want to hear.

Bless their hearts. There are people who walk among us who say unbelievable things. While it is true that, with widowhood, there is less laundry, fewer dirty dishes in the sink, and more closet space, bite your tongue before making such comments. That no way balances the scales against meals for one, nobody to cuddle with on cold or stormy nights, no wide chest and strong arms to hold us, traveling alone and doing all the heavy lifting, and bug squashing.

I don't mind folks asking me what is acceptable to say because it shows they want to help with the enormous hurt of losing a spouse. I am more understanding than many because my husband was often referred to by me as *Mr. Sensitive*. Years ago, when we met a new neighbor who told us about his heart trouble, Junior told him, "Heart trouble isn't as bad as cancer. Be glad you don't have cancer 'cause that stuff will kill you every time." Whereby our new neighbor said, "Well, I've got cancer too."

Please don't tell someone who just lost a spouse, "Don't worry. God has another husband waiting for you." He well may, but now is not the time to bring it up. Think about it. When your dog dies, do you want to run right out and get another one? Since it takes most people a long time to get over losing a pet, what are the odds they will be eager to marry again quickly? On the other hand, some people over age fifty have told me they feel pressured to start looking for a new mate because at their age, they are running out of time.

It may sound comforting to you, but do not say things like "Well, he/she's in a better place." True, but the surviving spouse is not in a better place, and they are feeling pain, misery, loneliness, loss; and a huge black void envelopes them. So please don't voice what you consider "comforting" platitudes until you put yourself in that person's reality.

We knew my husband was better off in heaven, healed rather than suffering with cancer; but at his funeral, his mother was quick to tell several people, "Don't tell me he's in a better place! He's not here with me!"

I could only say, "Amen."

Faith absolutely played an extremely important and indispensable role in making it through the death of my life partner. When those who crawl in bed with their spouse each night attempt to accuse us of loss of faith or lack of spirituality because we are actively and publicly hurting from our loss, it is a travesty and a total lack of compassion.

I believe I can honestly say that I never questioned God's sovereignty, but I do have a new fatalism because, after all the prayers that were offered up and so many people claiming the healing powers of Almighty Jehovah for my husband, it is with a new attitude that though I accept God's will, at this time, I also feel powerless in that faith. Until Junior died, I felt lifted up by the assurance of God's love. But after he died, there was a feeling of betrayal, which I knew to be wrong; but it was the way I felt. God knew it, and I couldn't hide it from either of us.

This is at odds with the certain sureness during Junior's cancer and since his death that the peace of God is holding me up; but regardless, it is the truth of my feelings, and certainly admitting such a thing will be frowned upon by some people. (Again, those feelings and that perception may change with time, but this book is about emotions and attitudes of the newly widowed.)

Normally, I can listen to people give advice with the best of them. I listen and accept what I believe and ignore the rest; but during this time, I had to restrain myself from jack-slapping a few people who dogmatically *shared* with me their opinions on how a new widow should think and act. (Let me say right here that I can imagine the reader-brethren groaning, "Oh no! She didn't just use the non-Christian term 'jack-slap.'" But let me remind our readers that even God's own children sometimes feel the urge to do bodily hurt to others. And if they deny it, I would also throw in the word "hypocrite." It is a testament to my faith that I was able to restrain myself, so let's move on. Christians are not perfect, but we are forgiven. Hallelujah!)

The truth is that there is not going to be a supernatural restoration of my marriage, and that reality takes some getting used to without having people pointing out every wrong thought and judging me for not being their idea of a good little widow.

When you communicate with someone who has had such a major life loss, remember that "I'm sorry" is adequate without being offensive. Keep it simple. Keep it nonjudgmental.

Chapter 3

REALIZE DREAMS LOST

A widowed friend sent me a card that says, "The future is a phantom seeking to spook you," and that's pretty much the truth because one of the hardest aspects of being widowed is the loss of the dreams and plans the two of us had for the future: plans to rock our grandbabies while enjoying the blessings of the rock of ages and traveling in our RV with friends like we so enjoyed doing. In its place is uncertainty and ignorance of this new place in life—though with God's help, we will get there one day; but we aren't there yet.

It's hard to admit, but many of us (at least for a while) don't really care about the future anymore because we feel like our life is over, and our former life *is* over. But because we have family and friends who expect us to hold up and carry on like the good, brave, and obedient Christians we claim to be, then we force ourselves to get up each morning and not only face another day but get through it with a smile and purpose. Our duty before God and people inspires us not to give in to depression or give up on surviving, although I don't always do it with grace. Sometimes there are tears and whining and complaining.

The way we see ourselves and the way others see us take some getting used to. I received a shocking revelation at the first wedding I attended as a widow. When the bride got ready to throw the bouquet, I was told to join the single women who were going to try and catch it! Who, me? Why would I be included in that group? I was slow to comprehend, but I am a single woman now, a single woman who still feels married.

One widow told me that after her husband died three years ago, she would fall on the ground in her front yard and scream and scream. I know a widower who frequently laid for hours upon his wife's grave and cried for the future that is lost to them as a couple. Another widow says she is waiting for her grandchild to grow up, and then she is going to step in front of an eighteen-wheeler. Hopefully, she will change her mind between now and then, but these are just some of the extremes that grieving people go through. Who is to say what is "normal" and what is not? Now that I have experienced what they have, I don't judge.

I have felt the liberating absence of fear of death that other widows and widowers have shared with me. Whereas I never thought I could stay by myself at our remote mountain home after Junior died, I discovered I had a new mindset that had me thinking, *So what if some axe-toting murderer does break in and hack me into little pieces? I'll just go on to be with Junior and the Lord sooner.* And with that comforting thought, I was able to go to bed and sleep without fear. I know it sounds gory and horrible, but I'm just telling it like it is.

"I drove up to my house one night, and there was a strange pickup truck setting in my driveway with three men in it," a widower told me. "I knew they could be there to rob and kill me, but I pulled in beside them and got out because I thought if they did kill me, well, I'm ready to go be with my wife."

This absence of the fear of dying may go away in time as life becomes worth living again; but over and over, I'm told that this feeling is typical and, in fact, is shared by those who have lost children too. Obviously, it is not something that most people go around voicing for fear they'll be locked away in a psychiatric ward, but it is real. And we don't want to hurt our family members by telling them this. These are *not* thoughts of suicide; it is just the absence of fear about dying when you know loved ones are there on the other side of life's veil waiting for you.

Most baby boomers can remember the song "One Is the Loneliest Number." Sadly, that is too true. As one Shreveport, Louisiana, widower, Glen Dale Miers told me, "You find out it is a couple's world."

I had told my husband before he died that I wasn't going to like being a widow, and I was right. I don't like it! The best thing that can be said is that I'm trying not to be a whiny widow, wallowing in my grief and pain while spreading the misery around!

There are exceptions. I have heard of "merry widows" who merrily discuss trips and cruises they are taking now that their cranky, unadventurous spouses are gone. (I'm guessing they did not have happy marriages.) One woman related how her husband had insisted she cook every meal for forty years; but since his death, she eats out every day and loves it. Admittedly, these are women of a certain age, my generation and older, who did what their men told them to do. I don't think the typical yuppie-aged wife has the same obedience training.

Every couple has their own special ways of dealing with each other. My husband was an alpha male, and our personalities were exact opposite from one another, kind of like the innate differences between male and female, which show up more distinctly when there are tires and a steering wheel involved. For example, once when my husband and I were on our way from our Louisiana home to Toledo Bend lake, I was pulling a ski boat, and the father of our children was pulling a camper. He insisted on driving behind me in case I "ran into problems." I thought my biggest problem was him driving behind, critiquing me.

When we arrived at our destination and during the days we were there, he kept complaining that I had driven too slowly, rode my brakes, and held up traffic. When we got ready to go home, I urged him to drive in front of me so he wouldn't be held up by my brake-riding, slower driving.

"No." He insisted he needed to follow me and for me to put the cruise on 60 mph and not take it off till we got back home. That's what he said: "Set the cruise on 60 mph, and don't take it off until you get home!"

So I did.

I lost sight of him in the first town. I had a green light and cruised on through, but he caught the red light, and apparently, *he* was obeying the speed limit signs. I tell you, that boat was swaying this way and that way, and there were a few times going around curves when it tried to go in a different direction than I was headed, but it hung on. I had set the cruise just as Mr. Driving Instructor told me to do. And like the obedient wife he wanted, my foot did not touch the brake even when it looked like our boat was going to get ahead of me on a straight stretch. Thankfully, it was Sunday morning, and the highway was nearly deserted.

According to the policeman who finally got my attention and dramatically indicated he wanted me to stop, he had chased me for miles with lights flashing. I was concentrating so hard on staying ahead of that boat that I had not noticed him. He could tell I hadn't deliberately ignored him, so he wasn't mad at me, and he kindly shared with me about how money from speeders is what provided his small town with the income to beautify the landscaping around their single flashing light. He also mentioned in the course of our conversation that as he tried to go around me to get my attention, the sashaying boat nearly sideswiped him.

Apparently, the town has a law, or maybe it's a state law, that speeders have to pay cash at the time of the violation instead of them sending you a bill. He wanted money for the ticket right then. But I explained about the obedient wife thing and how I was just doing what my hypercritical husband insisted. Once he understood that it was all the "big bossy man's" fault that I cruised through town at 60 mph, the nice policeman was laughing so hard he had to wipe tears away. He said it reminded him of why he was divorced. I asked the officer, and he agreed to stop my husband and make him pay my fine since it was all his idea. I gave the nice policeman a very good description of our truck and camper, so he wouldn't miss my fine payer. Then I continued on home at a slower rate of speed since I was pretty sure Junior wasn't going to be catching up with me any time soon. I certainly wasn't going to wait there for the deputy to pull him over so he could pay my speeding ticket.

I was pretty dang sure the conversation wasn't going to be sweet and loving.

Sure enough, when my complaining half pulled in our driveway an hour behind me, he wasn't in a very good mood. His reaction was typical of the way men view things. I did exactly what he told me to do, yet he didn't seem to appreciate it one bit, and his attitude about that nice cop was not the least complimentary. He never did tell me how much the ticket was; but on the other hand, he didn't follow me when I pulled the boat anymore either. He just headed out on his own and had faith that I would show up in my own sweet time.

Back when Junior was living, I always counted on him to have my back! Even if he was upset with me, he always came through for me. He actually took road signs at face value, whereas there have been times when I sorta use my own judgment about when road construction signs should be heeded. A number of times, I've gone around barricades and gotten out to move road closed signs that seem to have been forgotten by road crews, or else the road fixers just get a kick out of making people drive the longer "detour" routes.

I admit, there was one time when I should have taken the "Road Closed" signs as being there for a legitimate reason. Work on Dean Road in Shreveport had been going on for way over a year, and I was running late on my way to hosting a baby shower. The house I needed to get to was five houses off Dean Road on a side street, but road closed signs were up where I needed to turn onto Dean Road. I faced a dilemma because if I went all the way around Walker Road to Colquitt to get to my destination, I was going to lose precious minutes; but if I just circled around those road closed signs and drove a half mile or so down the formerly black-topped but currently muddy, red-dirt road, I could save valuable time. That was the plan.

It was a rainy Sunday afternoon in December, and I could see abandoned road working machines way, way down Dean; so I figured, if those machines could drive on the dirt, so could I. After all, as a hostess for the shower, I had strawberry pineapple punch that needed to be on time. So I gave my female logic full reign and got out and moved one of the signs just enough to let me pass through. I soon realized though that what looked like harmless mud was actually slick, muddy, clay-like substance that caused my maxivan to slide around. I had trouble staying in the middle of the road. Who would have thought that professional road builders would have topped a road with slippery red clay? The rain hadn't helped matters either. But as it was too late (and impossible) to turn around, I just aimed the van straight ahead and hung on until I slid off the road into a water-filled ditch. At least it was pretty close to the street I needed to reach.

Getting out of the van was exciting. I tried to stand on the running board to open the back door to get the punch bowl out; but in all the skidding around, a lot of mud had gotten thrown onto the running boards, so I ended up slipping off into the ditch. I sat there a while as the shock of chest-high, cold, muddy water soaked through my Sunday dress. It gradually occurred to me that I should have removed my high heels first because they were stuck in the mud and filth of the ditch, and I prayed that all the snakes were hibernating. It also crossed my mind to hope nobody was looking out their windows at me.

Eventually I got up from the ditch water and got the back door open, still standing in the cold, muddy water. With the way the van was angled downward, I had to get my short legs up the slippery side of the ditch and climb into the van to get the punch bowl. Everything attached to me made it onto the running board except my shoes, which were stuck somewhere in the mud, snaky-looking grass and chilly water. It took a few tries before I could get my wet, slippery arms around the sloshing punch bowl without sliding back down to sit on my rear end in the ditch again. I was still imagining there were a host of snickering people watching out their windows with good intentions of helping me once they stopped laughing, but nobody showed up by the time I climbed out the other side of the ditch, holding tightly to the heavy, sloshing bowl of liquid refreshment. I didn't bother locking the van or shutting the door because my main priority was getting out of the muddy, water-filled ditch without losing the heavy punch bowl; and it took both arms to hold onto it.

I walked barefoot, not counting the sagging, soaked pantyhose, past the first four houses looking like the victim of a tsunami; pieces of fruit and punch mixing with the muddy water running down my formerly Sunday best dress. Finally reaching my destination, I rang the doorbell with an elbow and stood there dripping till the other hostesses opened the door, wide-eyed but sympathetically understanding about the shortcut I took on Dean Road.

They took the crystal punch bowl to the kitchen to clean the mud off it while I went directly to the shower. I had to borrow some dry clothes from the woman of the house, which was a problem since she was eight inches taller than me; but at least I was covered and dry when guests began arriving. None of us were particularly surprised when the doorbell rang, and my cousin, Sharon, stood there with her muddy shoes in hand and red clay up to her knees.

"I could see Elaine's van parked down Dean Road, so I thought it was okay to drive around the road closed signs…" she starting explaining.

It made perfect sense to us women why Sharon decided to ignore the road signs, but explaining to our husbands about why they needed to come pull us out of the ditches on a closed road… well, let's just say that our men lacked understanding and sympathy.

It was unfortunate that when other people saw my van and Sharon's new sports car on Dean, they thought it was all right for them to go around the signs too. And then when our husbands came to rescue our cars, they had to call in reinforcements because they got stuck. Junior blamed me for everybody else's getting stuck and sliding into the ditches. By the time it was over, there was a whole line of vehicles slimed and stuck on Dean Road that Sunday. Apparently, when residents (mostly women) of the community who had been having to detour to get home saw our cars on the road, they thought, *Oh, the road must be passable now*; and here they came. It was a mess! It was also a learning experience. And when I told my husband that now, before I drive around road closed signs, I make sure the surface is dry and hard. He just shook his head. How could I not miss a man like that?

Coping

You can't be married for nearly forty years and lose that part of yourself without missing him in the extreme. I liken it to losing half my body or at least an arm and leg. The Lord helps you through it, but you still have to learn how to walk and get by without an arm and leg. When we were together, we saw humor in nearly anything; but without him, there is little humor. I smile and laugh, but my heart is not in it, which is all normal for grief processing according to the books, not that knowing that helps.

They say time heals; so I'm just going through the motions, hoping that the healing comes soon because, right now, the wounds are raw and bleeding inside where my heart was torn asunder. The outside is only a faked facade. Sounds pretty depressing, huh? Wait! That would be because I *am* depressed.

After Junior died, I rarely send out emails or posted on FB, and people were always asking why. There just wasn't much to say except that I wish I had been more helpful and sympathetic to the widows of my acquaintance, including my mother, mother-in-law, and sister. I felt like I had lost my humor. And if I'd written any updates to my friends, they would have consisted of tales of woe relating to things like how being short was a much bigger problem without my tall husband around to reach things for me. When the light bulbs went out, I had to wait for a tall person to come over. I can't screw a water hose on the faucet without it spraying water all over the place, and I can't till the garden without the tiller going off on its own because I can't keep it in the row. Getting a mower or tiller started is a challenge. There were many things I was realizing that I was useless at doing in the realm of Junior's former man chores.

When the weather was beautiful, I wished that somebody would come over who liked to fish and would clean the fish. Junior and I would ride our four-wheelers down to the lake to fish when the weather was cool and clear. Not only do I not clean fish, but I don't take them off the hook either. The one time I tried, I swear I heard the fish scream because I mangled it so badly. And since it upset me, Junior never asked me to try it again, and I never volunteered.

Things are always happening, and I turn to tell Junior about them; only he isn't there. I wake up early to watch the sunrise from our back porch, but it is not so pretty when you can't share it with somebody. At night when we used to go to bed and discuss the day and make plans for tomorrow, now it's just another *used to do*. There are so many things that married people don't realize how much we will miss sharing them when that other person is gone.

Marian Poe eloquently shared her coping mechanism in widowhood, "After Dave died, I learned to be grateful for the end of each day because there was no way I'd have to live it again. For me, the dreams of his return and the waking up at 3:00 a.m. to find the dream was not true were the worst. To this day, twenty-three years later, 3:00 a.m. is still a witching hour for me."

I know exactly what she means because often I dream that Junior's death is just an awful nightmare. Then I wake up to remember that the nightmare is real. The overwhelming joy I feel when I wake up expecting to see my husband lying beside me only to have that joy turn to despair is a real bummer. I wonder how long these dreams will last.

Marian gave me advice for our fortieth wedding anniversary, which I would spend as a widow: "That day only lasts twenty-four hours. You will never have to pass that anniversary again. I didn't know we had a yard until Dave died. Gradually, the yard became therapy for my raging anger, loss of faith, which floated for a while, and black depression. It became the only time my mind chatter would still and allow me to concentrate on 'the moment.' Your tears are healing signs, Elaine—one drop at a time."

One widow sent me her feelings: "I try to stay so busy that I can't or don't think or feel. Thinking of the future is like watching a scary movie. It is a constant battle to trust in God's plan especially when I thought being a faithful Bible-reading/teaching/doing wife, mother, and grandmother *was* God's plan. Then there's this total life changer with no directions burned in stone—like I said, scary."

Edna Wheless told me that she still cried when talking about her husband, Jimmie, so she's about quit talking about him : "The kids have their memories, and I have mine, and we don't discuss them for we will break down, and ever it shall be.

"I hate being by myself. I've about adjusted to it, but that does not mean I like it," she continued. "I can't put in a light bulb without a grandson to help, can't pull the lawn mower to start it, so have to get someone else to do it."

As I've already mentioned, the reading materials that people brought to me were either preachy or a lot of psychology stuff. I wanted to learn about the real, actual facts on how this widowhood life affected genuine women I knew. I like to know what to expect. That's why I decided to write this book because, though it is too late to help me, there are new widows being made every day. And maybe, knowing what others feel and what helps them to get through this will be a blessing to them as they travel this painful path. It is a path that I refer to as the *other trail of tears* because that's what happens when we are forced to set aside all the plans and dreams most couples have together. There's a new world order we have to learn to navigate.

Expect widow's moments. When I got a notice for taxes, I went to the courthouse where two women were working at their desks. I showed one of them the paper they had sent me, and she asked how my handsome husband was because she remembered him trying to talk to her with his mechanical voice after his throat was cut out. As soon as she asked, I began crying and couldn't stop. I don't mean crying silent tears, I mean boo-hooing, heaving sobs. I finally got the words out that he had died, and I tried to apologize for publicly expressing my grief so loudly and messily. She began bawling too, and the other woman got us tissues, and then she also started crying. We were a blubbering mess when the door opened and a man entered, carrying his paperwork. He paused, looking around the room at each of us, and the look on his face said, "I don't know what this is about, but I don't want none of it." He twirled around and left, shutting the door behind him. We began laughing through our tears at the look on his face.

Some fortunate people have the ability to laugh under the worst circumstances. God's Word says laughter is good for the soul; and between the two of us, Junior and I did a lot of laughing. When I wrote *Hello, Darling* just a few weeks after Junior died, readers were constantly asking how I could write a book about cancer and death that was funny. The truth is that I wasn't trying to be funny. I was just sharing our trip down death's valley the way we walked it.

During our nearly forty years together as man and wife, we loved April Fool's Day. But we got to where we couldn't play successful jokes on each other, so we had to branch out a bit.

I married into a family whose women believe a baby's head can be reshaped by squeezing, rubbing, and molding it with their hands. The art of head shaping has long been part of Dowden family tradition. In their part of Louisiana, it was common for people to bring babies born with odd-shaped noggins to my husband's aunts for "shaping." It seemed a little unusual to me at first because I'd never heard of the practice; but as a newspaper reporter at that time, I was avidly interested.

My early observations were that parents were pleased with the results, and I never heard of any child left brain damaged as a result of being reshaped by the aunts.

However, five years after marrying into this family, I gave birth to a son with a *big* head. In an effort to spare readers gruesome details, suffice to say the doctor broke my tailbone so Daniel's head could be squeezed through the birth canal. The result was a baby who was sympathetically described as looking like an anteater!

"Anteater" is not a description to cheer a mother's heart, but my in-laws assured me that the aunts could round his head out in no time. That caused me a little worry because although I accepted the practice in theory when it was used on other babies, I was not anxious to have my son's head remolded/reshaped by human hands.

Sure enough, my husband's aunts were called in to *help* our "pore little baby with the anteater head." There was never a time I didn't grit my teeth, stand close by, and listen for a squishing sound as Aunt Irene and Aunt Rowena (both deceased now) worked on Daniel's pitiful-looking cranium.

And, yes, he grew up to have a perfectly shaped head, brain intact, except for temporary lapses common to being male.

All this information is needed to set the stage for the rest of the story. Readers also need to know that for a ten-year period, my husband and I opened our home to foster children; so it was not uncommon for us to show up with a new infant.

Then one day, we became adoptive parents to a baby capuchin monkey. We went to my husband's hometown of Anacoco to introduce Amos Rex to the relatives. Rex was only eight weeks old, so he had very little facial hair. At that age, capuchins really look more human than primate—cute in a monkey sort of way but not what you would call "pretty" in human terms.

We carried him like the infant he was, wrapped in a blanket, wearing a diaper, and holding a bottle. And it so happened that our visit was on April 1!

My husband called his Aunt Rowena from my in-law's house and told her we had a new foster baby whose head needed some work.

"Well, son," she told him, "I don't guarantee anything, but you bring that child on down here. I'll do the best I can for the pore little thing."

So we carefully tucked his long tail inside the blanket and drove to her house. My husband told her a sad tale about the baby's poor little misshapen head, and we could tell Aunt Rowena was eager to get to work.

She pulled back the blanket to get a look at him and jumped back a little, exclaiming, "Son! Son! This is the ugliest child I've ever seen. Bless its little heart! But give him here, and I'm gonna lay hands on him and do all I can to help this pore child!"

Bless her heart for being ever willing to help a baby in need. She gently took Rex from his (human) daddy's arms and began feeling his skull bones. About the time she decided where the molding should begin, his tail fell out of the blanket onto her lap! Aunt Rowena nearly fell off the couch.

By then I was feeling kind of bad about "April fooling" her and was hoping she had a good sense of humor. Then before her nephew could tell her it was a joke, Aunt Rowena laughingly declared a miracle would be needed for this baby because she could not do a thing about that tail, especially on April Fool's Day!

I feel healing mirth just remembering this. Thank You, Father God, for the blessing of laughter.

Chapter 5

EMPATHY

Widowhood is like having cancer in that once you go through the experience, you are more attuned to the feelings of others traveling down the same path. The ones left behind offer advice and share their experiences with us newly widowed. They can relate because they have already faced the same challenges, judgments, attitudes, and problems. I listen to those who have walked the path before me because I want to skip some of the pain and jump ahead of common mistakes made by the recently widowed. Some of us wish we had known beforehand what we know now so we could have prepared better for the present reality.

One woman describes her experience losing her husband as someone cutting out her beating heart like African tribes sometimes did to their captives. That's pretty gory, but it's also keeping it very real.

When a spouse dies, people constantly ask what they can do to help. On behalf of the left-behind half of a couple, you can be available to lend a shoulder to cry on or an ear to listen sympathetically. Say, "I love you. Let me know when you want to talk or spend time together." Stay in contact even when the surviving spouse doesn't initiate the contact. They probably won't call or visit the way they did before because their mood and mindset is now ruled by grief and loss, and they may not want to bring anybody else down. But if you can take it, then spend time with him or her. Let them know it is okay to mention a loved one's name. Some people are obviously uncomfortable with talking about the deceased, especially men. Perhaps they fear the tears.

When I was around my husband's brothers after he died, I got the feeling that they were afraid I would talk about Junior and, of course, cry. I know they loved him and missed him because he was their older brother, and they all were close in life. They were a big part of our lives, and we often took them with us camping, scuba diving, snow skiing, and Dicky, born when Junior was nineteen, went with us to Disneyland. Perhaps I just imagined it, but that is what I felt. At Marze family dinners, we always held hands for the blessing, and I couldn't help but cry every prayer after he was gone. While my sisters-in-law patted my shoulder in unspoken sympathy, the brothers went the other way. I guess it is a man's way of emotional avoidance. I'm not a big hugger, but sometimes I wanted one of them to just let me hug him, soaking in that Marze persona, taking what comfort I could.

Some widows have told me that they yearn and ask for hugs from anybody with arms. They need the physical contact from being held close to someone's heart. Maybe, for a few seconds, they can pretend they are being held by their late spouse. Others, like me, shun a lot of hugging. I don't know why. During a memorial service at the hospice home where my husband spent the last four days of his life, I was standing alone, crying silently, and a stranger came up to me, saying, "You need a hug, and I've got one for you."

"No, I don't want a hug," I said and turned away. It was rude of me, and I felt bad about rejecting this kind stranger; but at that time, physical contact brought me pain. I can't explain it.

I'm not the only person to say that comforting words and hugs can cause emotional breakdowns. We can finally get control of the crying, and then somebody comes up and says something sweet about our departed one, and there the dam of tears bursts open again. Some people are okay with crying a lot, but I'm not; so that is probably why I shun a lot of comforting, especially in public.

For two and a half years, my husband told me, "I can do this terminal cancer with the Lord's help if you stay tough. But if you cry, then it's going to break my heart, and I won't be able to handle it." Over and over he told me, "You gotta be strong so I can be." I think all that being tough and strong kind of set in, so now I feel guilty if I let go with the tears.

The first time I went to a function among my husband's big family, I cried all evening because it was just overwhelming being with them and seeing the void where Junior should be. Other widows tell me they understood, so I assumed my reaction was typical.

Friends and family who have the patience and time can help a widow or widower by listening to the fears, lost dreams, and plans that will never come true now. It can be soul cleansing just to put those fears and loss into words. For me, the writing probably does what verbally sharing does for others. It's kind of like birthing stories where, thirty years after giving birth, some women can still expound in great detail about her pain and labor. Some people are still talking about losing a loved one decades later. And though the telling of it probably unloads some of the hurt and misery of loss, I am currently trying not to unleash on my acquaintances the tragedy of my widowhood. I figure, you have a certain window of opportunity when it is all new, and friends will listen patiently; but after that, it is only other family members involved who are going to want to listen.

It helps to focus on what is right, good, and beautiful in our lives to count our blessings. Friends who pray, call, visit, send cards, and plan fun excursions, like a movie or lunch out, are to be treasured. Learn from me though that when you go to a movie, go to a happy movie. My friends, Carter and Denise Sanders, invited me to attend a movie with them after Junior died; and since I was tired of crying and being alone, that seemed like a good idea. We went to see *War Horse*. When I walked out of that theater, I couldn't breathe for hours because I cried so hard over what happened to that horse.

Bobby and Billie King were one of our RVing couple friends, and Junior and I went on numerous full-filled trips with them.

Shortly after Billie died, Bobby made a trip with several of us couples; and late that first night when we left the campfire meandering back to our own RVs, Bobby went to his alone. When he got to his truck, I saw him break down, crying, and my heart hurt for him. I never forgot that incident. I felt the pain of his loneliness through his sobs. I thought about that incident a few years later. It was on New Year's Eve after Junior died in October 2011. I was staying in our motor home parked at Donnell and Bonnie Byrd's, and they had given a party attended by many of our friends. When the party broke up, and the couples began leaving together, I thought of Bobby as I made my solitary way across the yard to my RV. This time, I knew exactly how he must have felt.

The only answer I have found to counter the tremendous loss and despair of widowhood is that the Holy Spirit lives within us, providing us with His peace and comfort as stated in John 14: 26–27. How those people cope who do not have the sustaining power of His spirit in their lives, I just don't know.

Divorced friends often say that their separation from their spouse must be like a death. Annette Johnson emailed Junior a message not long before he died. "I told him how lucky you were to have such a loving and faithful husband," Annette told me. "His reply was, 'I'm the one who is lucky to have her.' That has stuck with me, and I have thought about his response so many times since. How very precious it must have been to have that kind of love."

She went on to say that she could relate to the emptiness, sadness, and loneliness. But as an unwilling divorcée, she did not have the comfort that comes from having known such faithful love. "It is my heart's desire to know the kind of love you were blessed with before I leave this earth," said Annette.

If there is ever a time for friends to share a positive testimony, it is after the death of someone's spouse. Cindy Moss Dowden lifted my spirits when she wrote me, "You two have been such an inspiration to me, especially in your marriage. I learned from y'all that marriage is just plain fun when you're truly in love with your life partner. I've always admired your undeniable passion for one another… Thanks for that. You both are inspiring to so many…"

For a Christian, it always comes down to God's role in our lives. We have a host of biblical examples of people who survived tragic occurrences for a purpose, such as Joseph and Daniel. Christian character is usually not developed in the good, easy times; it is the dark times of hopelessness that we reach out and hold on to our heavenly Father. When we can't change or control a situation, that's usually when we call out to God and cling to our faith. I cling like a monkey.

When I say I cling to God like a monkey, I speak from experience having owned monkeys for over twenty years. Capuchins have prehensile tails, which means they use their tails like an extra hand so that when they wrap themselves around your neck, arm, or leg, you may feel like an octopus has you in its clutches. Normally, that's a cute, cuddly monkey characteristic. But one day, Amos Rex, a capuchin monkey, was riding on my shoulder with a leash attached to his halter, and the other end was tied around my wrist. Our house had a pond on one side of the five-acre lot.

We were strolling down the sidewalk one cool, fall day. I didn't have my contacts in, so when I bent down to pick up what I thought was a tree limb newly fallen across the sidewalk, I realized, when it raised its nasty reptilian head, that it was not a limb. I screamed long and loudly. Monkeys are not afraid of much and can be very protective of their humans, so Rex jumped off my shoulder and snatched up the four-foot-long snake while he was still attached to me. Once he had a hold of the snake, he began climbing up my body with the snake flopping against me at the same time I was jumping, running in circles, flapping my arms, trying to get the leash unwrapped from my wrist, screaming like a lunatic at Rex to release the snake. My hysterics just upset and confused him. The snake wasn't liking being hugged by a monkey either, and it was coiling, hissing, and trying to get loose; but Rex was determined to keep his prize. I was frantic, hyperventilating, and was making laps around the yard and house, trying to get away from Rex and the snake, leaping and jumping (according to the neighbor's accounts). By this time, some of the neighbors had come to see what all the shrieking was about, and a couple of the cowards turned around and went the other way when they saw it involved a big snake dangling around my neck. Rex wouldn't let go of the snake and had his tail, feet, and arms clutching my head, neck, and the snake. So on my fourth trip around the house, I headed for the pond because Rex hated large bodies of water. He loved taking a bath inside the house but not lakes and ponds, so I figured that if I jumped in the pond with him, he'd let go the snake. But the smart little guy realized where I was headed, so right before I dove in, he finally dropped the snake! Hallelujah! The snake and I speedily slithered/ran in different directions, and I don't know about the reptile, but this woman was still freaked out.

Not only were my neighbors cowards, but they were also cruel and insensitive, unable to stop laughing while I was shaking and crying. I'm sure it was funny watching me leap, run, and jump, trying to disengage from a monkey and a snake, but still…

Chapter 6

Financial Issues

Financial issues and all the paperwork that comes with a spouse's death can be overwhelming. My husband had a preplanned funeral, but there were some unexpected bills and unforeseen problems regarding financial matters that shredded my nerves, and that's not really easy to do. It's a common situation for widows.

In addition to the general stress of all the costs of funerals, travel, and making difficult decisions all alone, I'm sure I'm not the only woman whose husband's checks were electronically deposited only to be electronically undeposited because they don't pay "in month of death," which really made things tight financially the first months.

A few days after my husband died, I stopped to get gas, and my credit card didn't work. Thankfully, I had enough cash to pay for the gas, or I don't know what I would have done. I didn't find out the reason why my card wasn't accepted until the next day when I called Discover because it happened on a Sunday when I was on my way back to Arkansas. I kept telling the attendant that the card was good, but she looked disbelievingly as if she had heard that story too often. It turned out that Discover froze my account because they found out my husband died, and I had to apply in my own name even though my name was on the card. It took weeks to reapply and get it in my name. So during that time, I had no credit card. It had been my husband's account, so it was like I'd never had a card before.

I was especially blessed to have friends and family who gave me money that I did not ask for in sympathy cards instead of flowers, which carried me over until things straightened out monetarily. Since then, I give cash instead of flowers in similar situations. All the trips to MD Anderson in Houston and costs of long hospital stays for cancer treatments had drained our savings account, and then the other checks we used to survive on were halted on notification of death. Oh yeah, it took four months to get the life insurance money! Be prepared by having cash on hand to last you a few months if possible.

In addition to hospital bills and insurance claims that bombarded me the weeks after my husband's death, another financial shock was when the city of Shreveport electronically took back my husband's October retirement check because they don't pay *month of death*. That was also when I found out that the 60 percent the city supposedly paid on our health insurance does not extend to widows; so what Junior had figured I would be paying for insurance was dramatically increased when I was required to pay 100 percent of it, instead of 40 percent. Junior was a retired captain with the Shreveport fire department and EMT (emergency medical technician). Thankfully, that policy of charging widows 100 percent has since been changed; but for six years, I paid nearly $600 a month for health insurance.

It amazed me that Discover and other agencies found out my husband died so fast. It took nearly two years for my husband to get disability checks from the VA, but it only took a week for them to take their check back after he died because they "don't pay month of death."

Junior wanted to help me buy a new car the last couple months of his life because we had put so many miles on our vehicle going back and forth to cancer treatments in three states, but I could see he didn't feel like car shopping. At this time, he was having to take morphine. "Don't worry, baby, I'll do it later," I told him.

A couple months following his death, our son, Daniel, took me to a Louisiana dealership where he had found a car for me. He got me settled at the desk with the car saleslady and then left to go to work. Not a big deal to most, but Junior always bought our vehicles, so I wasn't comfortable as I filled out the paperwork and wrote a check for the required amount before driving the car back to Arkansas. Weeks later, I found out that I should have gone to the DMV to pay taxes in Arkansas on the car, which was a surprise to me. When I complained to Daniel that he should have told me about paying taxes and the amount of taxes to expect, he said, "I thought everybody knew that."

No, somebody who has never bought a car doesn't automatically know that stuff, and I also didn't know I had to go buy a license plate to put on my car. I assumed they would send it in the mail. But finally, some discerning man friend told me I had to replace the temporary plate. It is things like this that happen over and over again that makes me feel foolish and ignorant. But when you have been married for a long time to a man who takes care of all the business and financial matters, at the advanced age of fifty-eight, I have to learn things to survive alone.

Usually, in every couple, there is one who handles the money. Woe to the survivor if he or she wasn't the one familiar with the financial affairs. A widower, in his seventies, handed me his checkbook and asked me to write a check to myself for something he was buying from me. He said his late wife had taken care of the money, and he had never written a check before. I insisted on showing him how and warned him against handing another stranger his checkbook. (I think my husband was laughing from heaven about me showing somebody else how to keep their checkbook because that was *not* my role in our marriage.)

Renee Strange lost her husband to cancer too, and her advice for future widows is to be sure both your names are on the titles to any current vehicles: "My husband's car was in his name only. My SUV was in my name only. When he died, I decided to sell his car since I didn't need both vehicles. But I was told, no, it had to be included in the succession. Had it been in both our names, I wouldn't have had to wait for the succession to be filed. I was also not prepared for the cost of the succession. You need a cushion of cash, if possible, for afterdeath expenses."

Over the years, I've heard women complain that they don't know how much to ask when selling their late husband's tools, toys, and equipment. Well, now I can relate to that! My husband had a four-year-old tractor with a front-end loader and brush hog. I got the blue book value off the Internet and also asked our brothers and some men friends how much they thought I ought to ask for it.

I got estimates with thousands of dollars difference, so I was more confused than ever. Finally, I put out the word for bidders to just make me an offer, but when I got a couple offers, I was told by others that the bids were too low and hold out for more.

As if that confusion was not bad enough, I had a man call me and say he had cash money and wanted to come look at the tractor to buy it. "I don't know anything about tractors," he said, "but I just bought some land in the country, and I need a tractor." He also told me his favorite scripture was, "Look out for the widows and orphans…" so I thought that sounded good and told him to come on out. I was alone on the mountain.

He was a big man, and he jumped up on my husband's tractor and started stomping on the gas and brake while stripping all the gears. "Stop," I finally said. "It's in neutral." He took it out of neutral and took off speeding across the pasture. I didn't even know it would go that fast, and I was worried by now because if I knew enough to know it had to be taken out of neutral gear to go, but he didn't, that didn't bode well for the tractor. As I watched him making fast circles, he had the front-end loader going up and down in front while also raising and lowering the brush hog in the back.

"Okay," I finally told him, "if you want to buy it and tear it up, that's fine. But you need to get off the tractor until you pay for it." He got mad and said some ugly things before leaving. Obviously, he forgot his favorite Bible verse because he called me back that night to tell me that he had gone and bought a brand-new tractor with the money that could have been mine.

"I hope they gave you tractor driving lessons to go along with the tractor," I said as I wished him well.

I was advised by some people to auction off my husband's tools, fishing rods, golf clubs, etc.; but then other women who had done that told me that they didn't get much out of the auction prices, and they wished they'd just given it away to people who might have wanted something with sentimental value. I did give some items to family members, and my son-in-law stocked toolboxes from Junior's tools for each of the five grandchildren.

At this time, I'm trying to sell the tractor, three trailers, a boat, and sundry items because Junior told me to sell as soon as I could because the value will depreciate with time. And since the place is up for sale, I don't need to have to move anything extra. I'm keeping the four-wheel ATVs because I figure that as long as I have the mountain home, I'd better keep boy toys so my grandsons can play.

Knowing that Junior was concerned about me handling my money competently, several friends expressed concern about how I was dealing with the money and bills once Junior was gone. I tried to reassure them that everything was good, and I was handling my financial affairs. When one of those concerned couples came up to visit, I insisted on taking them out to dinner. I paid cash for the meal. The male half of the couple asked about my method for keeping my finances straight.

"It's simple really," I replied, "I just cash the checks instead of depositing them, and then I pay cash for everything until I run out of money. That's when I know it's gone."

I could tell, by his stunned look and stuttering, that he didn't think too much of my bookkeeping system.

Chapter 7

EXTREME REACTIONS

S ome widows told me that after their husbands died, they didn't bother to bathe regularly or put on makeup. I waited for the inclination not to bathe to hit me; but so far, bathing is still a daily ritual in my life—to the relief of family and close friends. I know a man who swore he did not change his clothes or underwear for two months after his wife died. His depression was too severe. I've also heard of children who considered committing a parent to an asylum because their mom or dad could not get control of their grief and even widows and widowers who contemplated suicide when their spouses died. A few have said they stayed in a depression, which affected their interest in hygiene and "dressing up" for months and even years afterward.

I didn't experience these types of reactions, so I wouldn't know what to say to somebody who did except that I would just give them time to come to grips with their present reality, along with a lot of emotional support. I've been told by friends that after their dad or mom lost their spouse, they were never the same. So I guess some people never recover from such an extreme loss. But, thankfully, that seems to be the exception.

My intense desire to crawl in bed and stay there was not nearly as excessive as some of these other reactions I've heard about. I was able to force myself to get up each morning and get ready to make it through another day. But then I had my daughter and her family who were frequent visitors during those first weeks after Junior's death. And my mother and numerous friends came up from Louisiana and stayed with me frequently; so I had a support group, which some people do not have.

One of the ways that I was blessed was having friends come for extended visits. They are so dear and close that I didn't feel like I had to entertain them. They went off on their own and toured the area, but they were there at night to keep me company, which was important because the nights are especially hard. These friends let me cry, whine, and lament my lost life. They sympathized but didn't quote scripture or try to tell me how I ought to be feeling. Basically, they were there if I needed them, but I felt no compulsion to put on an act for them. When my grandkids were with me, I did feel obligated to fake it because they were having a difficult-enough time dealing with the loss of their papa. They didn't need to see me fall apart too. I would highly recommend that friends who want to help a bereaved person simply provide the kind of no-obligation companionship my friends gifted me with because I will be forever grateful for their non-demanding, supportive presence.

The desire to socialize may diminish significantly, as is common, I'm told. I love people to come visit me, but I didn't want to leave home for a while. My desire was to get in the bed that I had shared with my beloved and cover my head with my quilt and just stay there, pretending he would crawl in with me shortly. I felt panicked about leaving my safe place where I felt connected to my husband, and others have told me they feel or have felt the same way. But I forced myself to attend church (after a few weeks) and go on outings with the grandkids.

Church was one place I couldn't go at first because I would lose my composure when people were sympathetic, patting, and hugging me. It's difficult to hold back tears when confronted with loving kindness. When I would break down crying, so would other people. So it was just easier emotionally to stay away from church for a while.

During my adult life, I've known a few folks who have panic attacks. During one of my first times attending church after Junior died, I accompanied my daughter's family to their church. It was a full house that day, and I was sitting in the middle of a long pew when I noticed that the row of ladies in front of us was *the widow's pew*. It hit me then that, like my widowed mother, I was sitting with my family instead of my husband, and my future was sitting in the pew in front of us—old ladies dependent on each other for fellowship and as lunch companions. My daughter said I turned white, and I immediately recognized I was having a panic attack despite never having had one before. The walls were closing in. I've got to get out of here, I told her. *Now!*

Widows and widowers claim that some of their friends leave them out of dinners, parties, and events once they are no longer a couple, though I have not found that to be the case in my own life as of yet. A male friend did refuse to accompany his wife when she visited me because he thought it would make me sad being around a married couple now that I no longer have a husband. It doesn't. Ironically, though, some singles say they do resent friends who still have their spouse, and they prefer to socialize with other singles so they aren't reminded of their aloneness.

"It reminds me of what I've lost," one widow told me about why she hated to be around couples. I *can* understand why she felt this way. When I've been around couples celebrating their forty-fifth or fiftieth wedding anniversaries, it has made me sad because through no fault of my own, I'll never have that. But I do like being with couples, though I have been told over and over by widows that couples will soon drop me from their friendship circle. Another reason that the male half of a couple does not accompany his wife when she visits a single woman friend is because he thinks they will talk about *women stuff* the whole time. That's my theory.

If for no other reason, I like couples to come visit because now I've always got a jar that needs to be opened or a box to put away on a high shelf or some little something that needs a man's touch or muscle. Some of my men friends bring their tools when they come to visit because they know there is a lot of upkeep on a country place, and they have a helper's heart for a manless widow woman.

Chapter 8

To Move or Not to Move

It is common for widows who live in rural areas at the time of a husband's death to want to move closer to family, friends, work, and/or shopping. Coming home at night to an empty house and no neighbors can be scary and magnify the aloneness. That was the last "undone" item on my husband's list of things to do before he died—to sell our home in the Ozarks so I wouldn't be alone on the mountain, especially in the winter. It was fun to be snowed in with him; it is not fun without him. The chores he loved, such as cutting firewood and brush hogging on his tractor, are just another problem for me. Understandably, the situation is different for men who may choose to stay in their rural homes after a wife dies.

Whereas one widow clings to the home where she lived and loved with her husband, others can't wait to change locations so the old memories won't haunt them. A few widows told me they remodeled their home or rearranged the furniture before they could "move on." Still others make moves that they regret later, which is why wise ones advise waiting at least a year after a spouse dies before making any life-changing decisions.

In my case, my husband had put our house on the market as soon as he was diagnosed as terminal. Two months after my husband died, I did rearrange my living room furniture because I kept turning to speak to Junior's recliner. I wasn't trying to erase his memory by moving his chair. But each time I looked that way, expecting to see him, only to realize he wasn't going to ever be there again, it intensified my loss. It was a move of self-preservation.

I can't compensate for the loss of my husband, but I can choose to try to have a more positive attitude and testimony because Junior would not want his family to stay in the dark place his death moved us to. He would want me to be strong in my faith and everyday life so that our grandchildren can build on how they see me handle life's adversities. Striving toward better emotional and mental health is essential for moving forward, and to not move forward is to stay in that dark place. As a Christian, I feel a responsibility to not always let the loss overcome my proclaimed faith.

When we realized what a battle we were going to have to wage against Junior's cancer, I found new homes for my young English mastiffs, which I bred, raised, and trained. I kept three of the older mastiffs because it would have been too traumatic for them to have new owners. But caring for them while we were away for surgeries and treatments in Houston also necessitated the need for dog care-takers, which was a constant problem. But the comfort they afforded me after my husband died was indescribable.

The oldest dog, Abby, died while we were at MD Anderson for one of my husband's surgeries, which was very sad for us. She had special status in our family because she moved to Nashville, Tennessee, with my daughter to watchdog for her and be her companion. Then when my son would drive fifteen hours to Colorado to visit when we lived there, he would pull over on the side of the road and take a nap. There's a lot of desolate territory along the route, so I would send Abby with him so she could protect him.

The other two mastiffs were eleven and twelve years old when Junior died, which is old for this breed of dogs, and they had gotten to where they couldn't get up or down the stairs and steps without falling. I saw that they were suffering, so I made an appointment to have Roxie and Hoss put down. Roxie lay down and died the day before she was scheduled to be euthanized. The dogs had been with my husband and me for many years and had been part of our life, so it was fresh pain all over again to lose their loyalty and companionship so close to Junior's passing.

The day after Roxie died, the whole family went to the veterinarian with Hoss. Phaedra, her husband, Clyde, and their three children were all with Hoss and me as he closed his eyes and lay his big head down one last time. Everybody except Clyde was blubbering, and his eyes were suspiciously wet. I told the crying kids that the next pet I got would be a pet rock because I didn't want anything else to die on us. They agreed. Two more ties to my beloved but former life were cut. The losses of our dogs compounded the emotional and psychological bereavement because of their connection to our former life.

Back in happier times of prewidow days, our English mastiffs loved to ride in the truck with us, but their massive drooling heads hanging over our shoulders had negative consequences too. Many a time, while my husband drove, I napped in my reclining seat, only to wake up to find one of our dogs was using my head as a pillow and drool cushion. Ugh!

On the other hand, since my husband had a tendency to camp our RV in wild, remote areas in unknown parts of the country, there have been times I was especially glad the dogs were with us. One time we were camped off a dirt road near a dam (alone) with no buildings or streetlights in sight nor any sign of human habitation. My husband was sleeping soundly (snoring loudly) when I awoke to headlights shining in the back window. Acres of empty space were available to them, yet a truck was parked right on our bumper. I could see three men inside when the interior light came on as they got out and moved toward us. The dogs were growling, but I kept them quiet until I slung open the door and let them loose.

Even when big dogs are barking friendly, they can sound like they want to eat sweet little old ladies. And though I couldn't see everything that went on, I heard lots of barking, snarling, and men screaming like little girls as they ran and jumped into their truck and spun out! When I called the dogs back in, they had wide grins on their faces to let me know they'd had a good time. Their macho master never stopped snoring.

Rest in peace, my faithful friends.

The day I moved into an apartment in Louisiana after selling my house in the Ozarks will always stand out in my memory as bleak. At the home we shared, my husband was all around me in spirit and memories. But moving into a totally new environment for the first time by myself in a place where he had not been was difficult. At an age where we should be comfortable in our home surrounded by love and family, I moved alone into a totally sterile environment void of personal connections, and it signified so many broken dreams. I don't recommend it. On another hand, I know that the move forced me to walk into that new life I'd been dropped into.

The pros of living in an apartment in town are that when the sink got plugged up, I picked up the phone and called management who sent a man to fix it. After Junior died, every time something broke or wouldn't work right, I had to hire people or bother my friends/family by asking them to come fix it. Another positive was that I was around people. If I begin feeling depressed, I can drive five minutes to the mall or call somebody who can be here in a few minutes. There is a library nearby and other public places. That's a good thing. But the reality is that when I come back to this apartment and close the door, there is just myself and the void. I spend a lot of time talking to the Lord, asking for courage to face each day alone and help in making decisions without a husband's counsel. And I also talk to Junior. He answers me too. I hear him in my head. Or it could be the onset of senility.

One of the dreams shattered for me is that Junior and I did not want to be city grandparents. We wanted our grandchildren to be able to ride horses, help us garden, and gather eggs like we did with our grandparents. With that in mind, we bought a big house in North Arkansas with acreage near a lake and ponds for fishing and swimming. Junior and I would load the grands up and let them help us cut four-wheeler trails through the woods. We wanted them to have experiences that not many children nowadays have. That was another reason I hated to move into an apartment where television and their iPads are about all there is for the grandchildren to do, and that is 180 degrees off from the life we wanted for them.

It will sound really silly and strange to city people. But for us, farm and country women, we think it is wasteful to throw food away as apartment dwellers do. When you live in the country, there are critters that eats everything city folks throw in the trash, such as potato peelings, apple cores, and meat scraps.

We, former wives who didn't do the bill paying, have issues when we are suddenly responsible for paying bills. A few weeks after I leased the apartment in town, I opened my front door and found an eviction notice taped to the door, saying I had not paid my rent. It said I had five days to move out of the apartment, and it really got my heart rate going. It was Saturday, and nobody answered the phone when I called the office. I'd barely gotten moved in and was already getting evicted!

Several hours later, I found a lady in the office, so I explained that it was not because of lack of funds that I hadn't paid the rent; it was sheer stupidity because I'd just not thought about it. I just assumed they would send me a bill. But she said that it is written in the contract that I bring the check to her on the first of each month. Well, who sits down and reads contracts? Junior, that was who. In hindsight, it probably would have been a good thing if I had read it.

I know how wrong that sounds, but I've never paid rent before, which is not a good excuse for forgetting, but it is the only one I have. Junior and I hadn't had a house note in twenty years; and when we did have one, he paid it. So I simply never thought about rent. I paid a deposit when I moved in, but apparently, they expect me to pay each month.

The apartment manager charged me a late fee. But considering that I nearly got evicted, I just paid it along with the rent and considered myself blessed to still have a place to live. I put out the word to friends to remind me to pay my rent on the first of the month. Otherwise, I figured I'll have to check into a nursing home where they do everything for you.

Chapter 9

COUNSELING

Some cope with loss through counseling with psychiatrists, church counselors, grief share groups, recovery therapy, or unloading on a friend's shoulder. There are a number of resources available for people who have lost their partners. I've not personally sought grief counseling, but others tell me it helps them. During those early months, I lived too far from any grief counselors to want to make the long trip to see them, so I just prayed, read, and quoted scripture for self-counseling. I am blessed to have numerous family and friends I can "share" (read *unburden*) my troubles with, so maybe that is why I'm doing okay without professional help. On the other hand, perhaps by some people's standards, I'm *not* doing well emotionally and psychologically. But compared to other widows I'm acquainted with, I think I'm doing okay. Or I could be just faking it really well.

Linda Jeffries of Eden, North Carolina, lost her husband on Christmas Day of 2009. She attends grief share groups and other counseling sessions regularly but says she's still not through grieving. "There are 'ambush' times where grief slips up on you out of the blue," she says. "I think I would be dead if I didn't go to GriefShare.

Grieving takes a long time. Each year, we have a banquet to remember our loved ones where doves and balloons are released."

"They say you can't go back, you can't stay where you are, and you must move on. Also, they tell us that if you didn't love, you can't grieve," relates Linda, sharing about what she's learned in counseling. "The hardest thing for me is to watch other couples and wonder, 'Why me?' It's hard getting the groceries in by myself or trying to do 'man things' on my own. I don't like cooking for one person, going to bed alone, and nobody to care whether I live or die."

Linda was widowed before me; so back when I was trying to comfort her by listening and pointing out how many friends and family members she has who cares about her, I really didn't understand what she was feeling. Unfortunately, now I do. It doesn't matter how much your kids and grandkids love you; it does not fill the void that a husband leaves when he is no longer there to love, protect, and be that ultimate helper, friend, and partner we all come to depend on when we've been married for decades.

I heard a preacher say one time that when a marriage is broken, either by divorce or death, it is like taking the pulley bone of a chicken and breaking it in two. The separation is violent and permanent. Personally, if I was going to use a visual image of a chicken to make my point, I would say it is more like when my grandmother used to kill a chicken for Sunday dinner. She would end up chopping the head off or wringing its neck while the body would be flopping around headless. That's what losing a spouse reminds me of. Our dead half is the head, lying at peace, and we, who are still living, are the chicken's body, flopping and flouncing all over the yard, trying to find our head. That may be too graphic for squeamish readers, but I'm just keeping it real.

Linda had a hard life before marrying her late husband, Shorty, and he took care of her and provided the security she'd never had before; so that's why I think she is having such a hard time dealing with his death. She is a loving, giving person who has had the props knocked out from under her life, and her friends should be patient and give her time to accept this huge change that doesn't include the protecting and nurturing arms of her late husband.

I think there is a perception that if we let go of all the pain, we'll be letting go of our departed one. Heartache and sorrow keep the husband or wife close to us because memories are that connection, keeping them alive in our heart and mind. A feeling of loving loyalty can be the tie that forever binds us to the memory of our beloved, and it may also keep some people from moving on with their lives.

*****

Barbara Evans Parker says her faith in an awesome God got her through her late husband, Len's, death from cancer: "My dying spouse, although we both believed he would be healed, was always planning ahead on what would happen to me after he was gone. His reassurance that I could handle anything because of my 'ginormous' faith did actually do that.

"After he was gone, my family, church, and friends were always there—sometimes too much. I never knew you could be loved *too* much, but that is how I felt, so much so that I left the country for a while just to be alone. It may have been selfish on my part, but it worked. The hardest part is losing your identity. I had to learn to be by myself and learn how to be *me*, not wife or mother, just *me*."

I understand the "too much" loving part. After Junior died, I had a couple people want to "take care" of me, and we had to come to an understanding. Yes, my husband did take care of me and make decisions for me, but it was a role strictly confined to him. I resented anybody else who tried to take his place and tell me what to do.

What Barbara was describing is difficult for those who haven't been there to understand because it sounds like psychobabble: "I've got to find myself." But it is very real. We "old" wives have spent many years living a role as wife and mother. That's who we become. Once our kids are grown, it is called "empty nest syndrome." But when we are no longer a "wife," there is no term for it, but the feeling is similar. It feels like the bottom has dropped out from under your feet, and you're falling into a black hole of despair and fear.

One of the hospice chaplains described widowhood to me: "You are beginning an exciting new chapter in your life, and you will be starting a bold new adventure." Bull! That connotes willingness or a desire to do something new, which isn't true in our case. Exciting new chapter? We have been unwillingly and bodily thrown into this new chapter or new adventure, and we are kicking and fighting against it. Supposedly, until we stop fighting and give in to what our lives have become through no fault of our own, we can't move on.

I found myself buying food at the grocery store that Junior liked, even after he passed, when I knew I wouldn't eat it. I laughed and shared with Phaedra how silly it was to be buying stuff for her daddy when he wasn't there. But for that moment, it gave me comfort. It was something I habitually did for him, and the normalcy of it made my heart happy. Go figure. I realized that instead of the security and comfort having Junior in my life had given me, I was greedily preserving bits of our former life whenever and wherever I could find them. It's just another of those things that only those who have walked in our shoes can understand.

"I think that you never stop grieving because a part of you is gone. You can't get that back ever. You just learn to go on in life and turn the sadness into joy, the joy of knowing that person and remembering the good times, knowing they are in a better place with no suffering when death happens," Barbara Ann explains. "There is no *empty* like that. When you have been on a roller coaster of emotions for months—highs and lows, good and bad, sad and happy—and all of a sudden, it's gone. You are empty. How can I make it? I don't want to make it. I don't want to do anything. But I must. I have a family and a church and friends who know the faith I have, and I can't let them down. I have a God who loves me and sustains me always. I feel sad for people who do not have a network of friends and family who love them and who love the Lord Jesus Christ. They not only supported me in love and prayers but financially as well. I still grieve, but I still *live* until God takes me home." (Barbara Ann is now married to Jimmy Parker who was also widowed. They live in Hornbeck, Louisiana.)

Jimmy and Barbara are a good example of two people who lost their spouses to death but reclaimed happiness when they found each other. They give credence to what some people have told me that "you'll never be really happy again until you find somebody else to love."

I've known several men who married soon after their wife's death even though they were devastated by their loss. There's a common saying that men can't live alone as well as women. Of course, in our age group, there's not too many men looking for older women, and there's a lot more widows than widowers, so the selection is slim, or that's what I keep hearing.

A few of my women friends married within months after their husband's deaths, but every one of them married somebody they'd grown up with or had a former relationship with. To marry soon after losing a spouse may be taking a big chance because of all the chaotic emotions bouncing around. I can see where it could be hard to determine real and lasting feelings from just wanting to reclaim what is lost, similar to rolling dice. Mostly, I hear single women my age saying that they would like to have a man friend to go out to dinner and a movie with. Like me, they can't imagine another great love in their life, but they are open to it if God should ever arrange such a match.

There's certainly not a set time to begin dating. Probably, most women are cautious enough to hesitate jumping into a new relationship while they are still struggling to come to terms with widowhood. And because I try to learn from those who have gone before me along this path, I am wary because some widows have told me I'm going to get so lonely for a man that I'll be jumping on strange men just to get a hug or something equally bizarre. That scares me. I don't want to get that desperate, but that's what I keep hearing. Also, people will say, "You're still so young that you'll find somebody else to love."

I don't feel so young, and Barbara was one of the ones who told me that when she married Jimmy, one of her worst concerns was the physical part of marriage. It is one thing being undressed with your husband when you are nineteen with a young body; but at our age, you have to realize that a new husband might either burst out laughing or throw up when he sees us naked, and neither option is apt to make an older bride feel romantic.

Because it hasn't happened to me, I wouldn't attempt to give other widows advice on new relationships, but I do resent the restrictions between myself and other men since my husband's death. Junior and I had single men friends whom we would invite to come over or go to dinner with us. Now that Junior's gone, I miss their company; but I feel restrained in issuing invitations because they might think I'm "after them." I miss their friendship but do not have the freedom to let them know I want to continue seeing them as an extension of a long-standing friendship. Other single women tell me they have the same dilemma because there are men they would like to socialize with and would issue invitations to them but don't want to give the impression of "chasing" them.

Martha Branim is the widow of a retired firefighter who died of brain cancer. "The doctor said maybe he would have two or three years, but Jim lived sixteen months," she says. "I felt like I was in a room with all the lights off, and I couldn't figure how to get out. I probably grieved more then than when he died. There were so many decisions that had to be made—what neurosurgeon, what cancer center, what radiologist, what oncologist to use while watching my husband of forty-one years struggle to do the daily activities he had always done.

"He had seizures, couldn't dress, feed, or bathe himself. I had to keep a smile on my face for his sake and our boys. I cried a lot in the bathtub. We learned to laugh at a lot of the obstacles, and he knew I would never leave his side, which gave him comfort. When he was in the hospital the first time, he slept on the sofa bed with me at night. I was his security blanket. The last month in the hospital, he couldn't talk or even open his eyes, but he knew I was there. I whispered in his ear that I was going to be okay. The boys were going to take good care of me. I learned to lean on the Lord, our boys, and our friends. God was so good. He always put the right person in my path at the right time."

"My hardest part of being 'left' is just being alone," explains Martha. "I stay busy. But when I go to functions, I am alone now. Jim and I were always together. It's like I don't really fit in. Even when I'm in a crowd, I am still alone. My boys and their families include me in their activities, and I'm active in Sunday school and choir. I'm learning to play guitar, and I keep busy, but I still miss him."

Martha is a good example of a widow who kept active even through her pain and loss, which is a good way to keep from being depressed.

When I go out and do things with people, somebody will say, "It's so good that you can still be happy with Junior gone." Actually, happy is a feeling I haven't had in a long time, but I just keep going and doing with the grandkids and work so that my mind and body are too busy to crawl into our bed and hide there. I'm blessed that Phaedra sings on a show in Branson, so that gives me somewhere interesting to go and new people to meet each week. I've met numerous widows at Phaedra's show who are traveling together, which seems like a great idea to me. A surprising number sold out and moved to Branson from other states because it is a tourist town with lots of jobs for older people and safe places to go.

Another avenue I have for keeping busy is my work. I write and edit business newsletters in addition to writing and editing a magazine. I have taken on an overwhelming amount of work that keeps me stressed but also prevents me from having time to give in to all the feelings of grief and loss on a regular basis. Basically, I try not to have time to give in to depression. Having a big place to keep up is also stressful but keeps me busy. *Busy* is good when you are trying not to think about a loss.

Glen Dale Miers lost his wife, Marilyn, to a brain aneurism, and he has spent a lot of time at the gym since then. He goes for morning water aerobics and then leaves for lunch with friends and returns in the afternoon for more exercise, or sometimes he just sits on a couch, watching television at the gym. The object is to be with people. Another way Glen fights against the loneliness is to sit outside his house in the sun and wave to people as they pass by.

"Sometimes the grief just hits you, zaps you when you may be talking to a total stranger," Glen explains. "I talk to people on the phone, especially at night, because it seems like your mood goes down when it gets dark. When the sun comes up, you get more chipper. I grew up with radio, so I keep the radio on at home. For some reason, Saturday and Sunday are rougher on me than the weekdays."

I, too, find that Sundays are very difficult because Junior and I always attended Sunday school and church together and usually went out for lunch with friends and had a relaxing afternoon before heading back for evening services. That routine was set in stone. So now my Sundays feel especially empty and lack decades of routine.

Glen also enjoys visiting his son's family in Baton Rouge, and sometimes he just gets in his car and travels all by himself. "Sometimes it is more lonesome traveling alone, so I turn around and come back home," he says. "But there are times when I've just got to go somewhere. It makes me feel better just to leave for a while. I don't think you ever get over the death of a spouse, though the pain eases some."

Chapter 10

HOLIDAYS AND OTHER SPECIAL OCCASIONS

Everyone knows that Valentine's Day commemorates the loving feelings between spouses, sweethearts, and lovers with sweet expressions of flowers, cards, and candy. It is the only day of the year that some husbands feel lovingly obligated to take their "cook" out to eat! Unfortunately, some people have lost their heart's valentine. For widows and widowers, a group of which I now find myself among, Valentine's Day can be a sad reminder of a lost love.

A large number of people have experienced the trauma of losing a spouse; and next year, there will be more husbands and wives who will be spending Valentine's Day without their sweethearts. So for those who are blessed to still have their valentine, hold him/her tight and make sure they feel your love.

Even April Fool's Day was special to Junior and me because we enjoyed playing pranks on each other and others too. It all began thirty years ago when I played a dirty trick on Junior for April Fool's Day.

The joke that began our spousal competition took an unexpected and undesired twist because it happened prior to everyone carrying cell phones.

My husband bought a bull and had been fattening it up with visions of steaks and hamburgers running through his head every time he looked at this steer. His family's philosophy about animals can be summed up as, "If I can't eat it, I don't want to feed it." They take their meat (or potential meat) very seriously. My philosophy is that if it has fur or feathers, I want at least one. So we have had a few conflicts over the years what with the pet monkeys, raccoons, squirrels, dogs, horses, rabbits, cats, and birds the kids and I have owned and fed.

Anyway, my husband and his brothers had been planning a camping/fishing trip for weeks, and he was *really* looking forward to it. He got up early on April 1 and left to meet them. Since this was before we had cell phones, he stopped at a marina nearly three hours later and used the pay phone to call and let me know he had arrived safely and would be unavailable for the next few days.

In one of those sudden, creative inspirations that April 1 seemed to bring out in me, I impulsively said, "I'm so glad you called because something's wrong with T-Bone (the bull's oh-so-original name). He's lying out in the pasture with his feet up in the air and hasn't moved for an hour."

"Well, go nudge him and see if he can get up. Check to see if he's alive," he yelled excitedly.

"No way," I replied. "He's liable to jump up and gore me!" (This was a *mean* bull!)

"You need to find out if he's okay," said hubby. "If he just died, we can still save the meat. And if he's not dead, we need to get him to the vet."

"You know he tries to kill me every time I go near him," I said. "I'm not getting close to that mean bull!"

I could tell my steak-loving hubby was getting more agitated, and I was just about to say, "April fool!" when he hurriedly replied, "Okay, I'm coming home. I'll be there in a few hours!" *Slam!* He hung up the phone!

"Wait!" I yelled to a dead pay phone at some unknown marina. Oh dear!

For the next couple hours, I was imagining how "unhappy" (that word is a major understatement) he was going to be if he came home and heard me say, "Sorry, honey, it was an April fool joke gone awry. Your bull is happy and healthy, so just turn around and drive back and enjoy your camping trip."

Normally, the man I married is slow-to-anger and enjoys a good joke, but this had all the earmarks of being one of those situations where things could get ugly. I actually contemplated tapping T-Bone on the forehead with a .357 round so he would be getting stiff by the time my husband got home. (I mean, the bull was going to have to die before we made hamburger out of him anyway!) But that troublesome bull wouldn't come close enough to the fence for me to get a good shot, and I wouldn't take the chance on wounding him and causing him to suffer. And I couldn't get close without him goring me. Did I mention he was mean?

Later, I heard my husband's truck throw gravel as he whirled into the driveway. He jumped out and ran into the pasture where his bull was munching contentedly on grass. I watched as my dearly beloved felt and examined T-Bone all over. I had explained to the kids what a neat April fool's joke we were going to play on Daddy, and as we met him at the pasture gate, he was asking, "What happened? T-Bone looks fine."

Remember, it was still permissible to lie because the day wasn't over yet, so I clasped my hands together thankfully and gushed, "It was a miracle, baby! We prayed that T-Bone would recover and be healthy and happy when you got here. And look at him now!" (Believe me, there had been some prayers offered up before Junior got home!)

The real miracle was that he believed me. After all, it *was* April 1! I eventually told him the truth much later, after I thought enough time had passed that he could appreciate the humor of an April fool's joke gone bad! Apparently though, I didn't wait long enough.

*****

My husband died in October of 2011, so Christmas came up too fast to prepare myself for the tremendous void—if such a thing is possible. I had no desire to decorate or bake or do anything festive. My daughter didn't feel like it either. But she has three little children, so she had to go through certain motions for them. I think it made it easier though when my son-in-law's parents graciously invited me to spend Christmas with all of them in Nashville, Tennessee. And though I appreciated the offer, I really wanted to stay at home by myself, crying and remembering the good times we had together, such as the Christmas we spent in Red River, New Mexico. But I knew my daughter and grandkids would be sad if I did that, so I forced myself to go have a *merry* Christmas. Was it easy? No. But I haven't done easy in a long time. And for my family, it was the right thing to do.

For Christmas or any holiday, it would be a real kindness to invite people you know who have lost a family member because they probably need to go somewhere different and be with people.

Some people tell me they can never celebrate holidays again after the death of a loved one, but I try to do it for the sake of the grandkids.

People keep telling me I need to think about what I need, not what my family needs. That may be true, and I'm not going to criticize those who think about themselves first. But selfishness has never been one of my motivating forces. I can't *not* think about how my actions reflect on and influence those around me, especially my precious grandchildren. When they see me outwardly grieving, it hurts them and makes them sad. That in turn makes me sadder, so it is a vicious circle when I give in to my feelings of loss and despair.

Also, I've known adults who mourn the loss of parents who withdraw from the family following a death. Where once they were a devoted grandparent, they become distant and uncommunicative to the little ones they once doted on. Children don't understand that, so this is another issue on which I have tried to learn and avoid in my own widowhood.

Not that I've avoided the need for isolation altogether though. There have been plenty of nights when Kinsley or Makenna wanted to spend the night with me, and I've had to tell them *no* (or rather I ask Phaedra to tell them "no") because there have been days when I was faking it in front of them, and I needed the night to just give in to all the built-up emotional turmoil without an audience. There are times when I have to be alone so I can be sad, or sometimes I just like to remember the good times, the fun times, the loving times.

As I write this, I am dreading our fortieth wedding anniversary coming up because we were planning to have a big blowout to celebrate. Yet I am thankful for the many we did have together, and joy truly fills my heart when memories of my husband come to mind. In weak moments, I yearn for his shoulder to lean on, his broad chest to cry on, and his strong arms to hold me. But in my saner moments when I'm tuned in to this new reality that is my present life, I try not to dwell on what once was because that way is to keep opening the raw wounds that his death created.

I am convinced that there is such a thing as a marital umbilical cord that is just as binding a connection as the birthing cord between a mother and infant. Even once it is cut, the emotional and psychological bond remains.

Perhaps the most difficult thing to do after the death of your spouse is to give up the illusion that you can ever go back to that former time. Perhaps it is an impossible task but one I feel I must keep trying to attain, which is to get it through my head and heart that there will never be a resolution of "what might have been" and "what should have been." It is what it is, and our choices lay more in what we might do to lessen the pain instead of eradicating it.

I'm hoping and praying that somehow, in the coming months, I will have a direction to follow in this future that I never envisioned for myself, just as each widow and widower has to do. I hope this book will be a help for others who, like me, have been seeking answers about this journey we have been forced into taking. Bless you as you make a new life and future for yourselves.

For that goal, I'm turning my attention to helping others or hiding my hurts beneath the antics and smiles of my grandchildren.

For myself, the overcoming presence of the Lord gives me the grace and strength to get through each day, and His promises comfort me.

> *These things I have spoken unto you, that in me ye might have peace. In the world ye shall have tribulations, but be of good cheer; I have overcome the world.* (John 16:33 KJV)

If there is a lesson to be learned from this book and these testimonies, it is that if you still have your loved one, hold him or her close because you never know what the future may hold or who may not be there for you to hold in the future!

> *Through the heart felt mercies of our God, God's sunrise will break in upon us, shining on those in the darkness, those sitting in the shadow of death, then showing us the way, one foot at a time, down the path of peace.* (Luke 1:78–79)

Book 2

Chapter 1

A Decade Later

I get requests for the *Widowhood* books almost every week even after eight years. But I'm out of books to send people, so they are paying extra dollars to buy them online. Some think that when they buy a book from Amazon that I get the money. That's not true. I assume, those books come from folks who sell their old books. Some pastors and counselors order fifty or so books at a time, which I cannot fulfill now. So I've done a reprint, plus I added an update. What was true when widowhood was new to me has changed somewhat, so I wanted to bring readers up-to-date while keeping the original "straight from the funeral" first book.

Second Introduction

A second printing of *Widowhood* was needed because I'm still getting requests for it, but the original publisher is out of business now. The first manuscript was written five months into my widowhood, and things change. Thankfully, life doesn't stay the same… in all ways. We don't stay in the same dark place forever after the death of our loved ones. Some of the changes need to be recognized, both for an honest portrayal of life without my husband and also to give hope to those new widows that the sun will come out again eventually.

But because the honest sharing of my early reactions and perceptions have helped so many widows and widowers, I'm letting the original *Widowhood* book stand and update from the perspective of eight years later. During this in-between time, I've interviewed numerous widows for magazine articles, and I've visited with many more at conferences, book signings, churches, etc. There's no right or wrong way to feel or an exact calendar on emotional highs and lows, but it helps to know you are not alone in your feelings. The sensitive issues that come with being the leftover part of a couple are stressful enough without thinking you are alone in the void that is widowhood.

The pain lessens. It is still very much a part of who I am, but it is subdued now. The void remains, but it is more a dull ache rather than a screaming pain. Maybe that is because overtime you realize that it does no good to cry and scream. He's gone, and that's not going to change. As years pass and that new normal turns into acceptance, I have learned to live with "what is" instead of "what should have been." Do I ever have times of crying, anger, and resentment of the former life I still miss? Absolutely. But the agony is not as prevalent. Eventually, I have moved on as so many advised me to do in the early days. There's no choice really. You either move on or die, maybe not physically but emotionally. Hopefully, this updated book will help new widows and widowers with moving on too. Unfortunately, not all claw their way out of depression, anger, and dependence. Years later, they are still locked in a dark house, avoiding family and friends, dependent on pills to sleep and wake, despondent and unable to function in a world they perceive as lonely and cruel, having stripped them of their reason for living. Sadly, I know several still wallowing in the emotions of recent widowhood.

*****

One of the questions I get from widows then and now is how long it will take for the pain of loss to go away. I'd love to say the hurt disappears in a year or two. The truth is that I've come to believe it never fully goes away unless they fall in love and marry again. Over the years, I've seen women and men who can't function after the death of a spouse suddenly become a new person when they find another special someone.

On the other hand, I've known several who jumped into another relationship, and it ends in a quick divorce or unhappy marriage. The explanation goes kinda like this: "I was so happy in my previous marriage that I thought another man and marriage would make me happy. But it's not the same."

In one too-fast marriage that ended in divorce between two very nice people, the man was still hanging on to what used to be. His new wife moved into the man's home after marrying. He was happy to have found another woman to love, but he became upset when she made changes in the home he'd shared with his late wife who had kept an open Bible on the coffee table, and he wanted it kept just like she had left it. He got angry when his new wife moved the Bible to another place. He also expected her to wait on him like his wife of forty-plus years, but that was not happening. So in only a few months, this couple knew they'd rushed into a marriage before the man was ready to give up his deceased wife. Some things just take time, but the loneliness causes some folks to *jump the gun*, as the old folks say.

The more years that pass, the more happy memories come to mind. You don't dwell on the dying as much; and hopefully, you've come to terms with the loss, and you have learned to deal with that void by filling it with work, family, exercise, or hobbies, like quilting or painting. But no matter how busy you are, there are still the holidays, anniversaries, birthdays, grandkid's graduations—special occasions that hit you hard. And *it* still hurts.

When our oldest granddaughter walked across the gym floor six years after her papa died, and I saw her dressed in a formal gown with makeup as she was crowned Homecoming Queen, I just began bawling because it was a moment in time that he should have been there to share. You think the sudden crying jags are over, and then—*wham!*—a new one hits you.

It has been years since my husband died, and I am still benefiting from his foresight in planning for his death and how his absence would affect me. One of the plans he set into motion for my benefit involved his loud, big, old, white truck. For his retirement from the fire department in 1999, my hubby bought himself a brand new 2000 Dodge diesel dually truck that pulled our fifth-wheel RVs during the next ten years we traveled across this country.

During the three years we lived in the Colorado mountains at an elevation of over ten thousand feet, there were times I drove what he called his big hoss to traverse rough rocky roads and several feet of snow. But when we moved back south to a less harsh environment, it wasn't my vehicle of choice. I could not get used to keeping the dually's wide "hips" within the correct parameters of narrow lanes. Knowing that I wasn't comfortable driving the hoss, shortly before he died from cancer, he gave the truck to our daughter and her husband with the understanding that when I needed anything hauled, they would get it done for me. He didn't want me to be burdened with upkeep and insurance for two vehicles, but he knew there would be times when I would need a truck, like when I was moving furniture and mattresses. When Phaedra drove up in this nineteen-year-old truck, delivering a big sheet of plywood to me, I was reminded of how, in spite of the terminal cancer her daddy was dealing with, he was looking ahead, trying to make life easier for me. Renting a truck to haul stuff is one less thing I have to pay to have done!

Even though Phaedra and Clyde have put thousands of dollars into mechanical upkeep over the past few years to keep the hoss running, they have been faithful to her daddy's wishes of making his truck available to me when I need it. And every time I hear that loud old diesel driving up, it makes me appreciate and be thankful for the foresight that has lightened some financial loads for me.

Once a woman is widowed, she starts paying for so many things and services that previously her husband took care of. And if you don't think people take advantage of a woman alone, you haven't walked a mile in our shoes. To some, having a truck available (and the muscle to load and unload) won't seem like a big deal. But to those of us who all too often have trouble finding someone ready, willing, and able to do what we need done, it is an important blessing, and I'm thankful for it.

In the years since he died, I've become adept at keeping a list of hired men who do house repairs, yard work, and handyman jobs. There's a group of us widows who share names and numbers when we find a good worker. I've been blessed with married friends, like Wayne, who came over with his chain saw when one of my trees fell across the street and Jesse who came to save my remaining goldfish from a snake that got in the goldfish pond and ate most of the fish. There are so many others who don't realize how thankful I am for their help. I'm just one of many who can use a helping hand.

*****

When Junior was diagnosed with terminal cancer, we faced it together. From that moment, we were forged anew with one purpose—to fight for his life against all odds and medical predictions. I was there for him. But what happens to the spouse left behind when they get bad medical news as so many of us do as we age?

When I was younger, I took my body for granted, assuming it would breathe, move, and function the way it was meant to do. But now that I'm in my sixties, I don't take anything for granted. Each morning I wake up is with the admonition, "Body, don't fail me now" right after I thank my heavenly Father for getting me through the night.

Having had altitude sickness several times while we were living in Colorado, I knew what was happening two years ago when I accompanied my daughter's family to our favorite ski slopes in Red River, New Mexico. Altitude was over ten thousand feet, which can cause altitude sickness. On my first day there, I had difficulty breathing. So while the family were all skiing, I was gasping for breath until the ambulance hauled me away to the hospital with an oxygen stat of 76 (not good). After spending the night in the emergency room on oxygen, the doctor told me to get to a lower altitude immediately, and no more mountains for me. I consider breathing a privilege, not a right.

Not breathing correctly can affect your heart in a bad way. After a round of tests (alone), I was told I have congestive heart failure (CHF) and should not do any activity that raises my heart rate over 100, including vacuuming and exercising. After listening to all the warnings, I left the doctor (alone) with the feeling that heart failure was only minutes away, and I should walk slowly and softly for the rest of my short life.

A finger monitor kept track of my heart rate, and it was hard to believe that the same heart that had served me well through premature births, five grandchildren, river rafting, and the cancer and death of my beloved husband would fail me now. Deciding I didn't want to sit around, waiting for my heart to peter out and needing proof that my life wasn't totally over, I promptly went for a horseback ride in the Ozarks better suited to surer-footed mules, which I decided, as we slid down rocky trails, is not for the faint of heart. When I survived that ride, I went with three of my grandchildren to experience a two-thousand-foot zip line across a deep canyon because I could not face a sickly future by myself; so I needed to test the perimeters of my health, so to speak.

That was my first time to zip line. I got to noticing that I was the only person over twenty-five paying to strap themselves on a hook attached to a cord, whizzing across the canyon floor 350 feet deep. About the time I was thinking I ought to rethink this heart-testing activity, the kid in charge strapped this big (in my case) diaper-like contraption between my legs and buckled it to a steel bar. I was concentrating on getting the diaper wedgies out of a critical area when he told me to lean back, and then he shoved me off the cliff. I remembered, as I sped across the treetops at jet speed, that he'd said something about the more weight you have on you, the faster you went. Immediately, the thought processed through my freaked-out mind that I really should have lost a few, or a lot, of pounds before getting on a zip line. I admit, I really hadn't given much thought to the mechanics of zip lining. But I assumed, while I was shooting across the canyon, that there was a brake to slow me down before my face planted into the granite wall at the other end of the zip line. But when I showed no signs of stopping or slowing, I began making my peace with my Maker because I knew that in a direct confrontation with solid rock at the speed I was traveling, my body was going to be splattered all over that mountain.

It turns out that there is a big iron spring at the end of the zip line that suddenly (emphasis on suddenly) catches right before up-close contact with solid rock. The landing was a shock to my body, a sudden, spine-wrenching, head-over-diapered-butt-flipping shock to my whole system. It was later that I figured out why my grandkids all insisted on going before me so they could be there to watch me land. I kept waiting to drop dead since my wildly beating heart rate was way over 100, and when I didn't, I came away with a more positive attitude about being diagnosed with CHF.

We all know the outward changes our bodies go through, but it was a revelation to find out that my insides aren't what they used to be either. My husband and I loved four-wheeling rough, tough terrains. I had my own four-wheeler, and we bumped and humped down some really ragged trails and creek beds—the rougher, the better. But after diverticulitis and kidney stones, my innards object to a lot of jostling and bumping. It brings to mind the times I've driven over rough dirt roads with "older" people in my car and how they held their abdomens, complaining about the roughness of the ride. Now I understand.

Fair warning, this is a subject on which I try to block from my mind because, if I think about not having the loving moral support when I'm in physical distress that I provided for Junior, it is enough to bring on a bout or two of depression.

Chapter 2

HARD ISSUES

Right after the death of a beloved husband or wife, *we* try to find a reason to get out of bed each morning. If a person is blessed to have family and friends, some of them may be generous with unrealistic (my opinion) spiritual advice that God our Father was going to wrap His strong arms around me, and I would feel no pain. I was told over and over to "count it all joy."

Understand me, I am a believer, and God gave me the strength to make it through the cancer and death; but you don't lose your God-given mate of forty years without feeling pain, loss, and grief. Hard truth is, I did not feel joyful in 2011, and I do not feel joy when I think of my loss. Joy that the Lord is with me? Yes! Joy that the love of my life, companion for forty years, father of our children, and Papa to our grandchildren who are growing up without him—*no*, I don't feel joy. If that makes me a bad Christian, well, it is what it is. This little book is being used in several states by doctors in their grief counseling and in grief share groups. And pastors hand it out to their grieving people. Why? Because people say, "This is exactly what I feel!"

My mother was widowed the first time when I was seven. She cried every day for over a year or so, it seemed to me, until she married again. She has now outlived four husbands, so I know there can be love after the death of a first husband. But it's now been nine years, and there's been no new love for me. I have observed many men and women moving on into new relationships, and I'm happy for them. But it seems like most over fifty singles do not get remarried, so it is just smart to learn how to deal with being unmarried for the rest of your life. I've said before that I prefer learning from others' mistakes so I don't make the same ones.

Ever since the first *Widowhood* book was published, I've had many readers tell me they insist some of their families and friends read it. "I want them to understand what I'm feeling. This little book says what I can't explain to them. I don't want them telling me to 'move on with your life' or 'toughen up.' It's my grief, and I'll move on when I feel like it."

Some readers have told me that the same issues affect divorced people and parents of children who die. Also, some people live alone because their spouse has had to go live in a nursing home due to dementia, a stroke, or some other debilitating disease. Many of us have left our homes and sweet memories and moved to a new town or state to be near adult children or for numerous other reasons. But the bottom line is that we would not be making the same moves if we were not living alone.

Prior to his death, I didn't realize I was dependent on my husband for so many things. He was a man who carried not only his load but mine too. So when he was gone, I had to deal with things I'd relied on him for.

I was driving with a friend on the interstate in August after Junior died when I saw what looked to be a big sheet of cardboard, and I tried to miss it. But 18-wheelers wouldn't let me over in the other lane, so I was forced to hit this cardboard at 75 mph. It turned out, it wasn't cardboard. It was a big, dead, bloated deer; and the clanging, banging noises of bones and antlers sounded like the underside of my car was ripped out. We debated on whether to stop and do an inventory of damage, but all the blood, guts, and gore were a huge factor in us deciding to just drive till the car quit rather than come face-to-face with the nasty stuff. My immediate thought was to call Junior and ask him what I should do. As always, the realization hits that he is no longer there to advise, counsel, or drive to get me. That's one thing that hasn't changed in all this time since he passed, the frightening knowledge that I'm on my own.

Back in prewidow days, I left Nashville, Tennessee, driving alone except for my monkey pal, Rex, and we got in a terrible snowstorm. Understanding that being from Louisiana snow flurries freak me out. But this was a real storm. There were more cars and 18-wheelers in the ditches than on the road. I was driving about five miles an hour, and other drivers would blow around me going 30 mph. But then later, I'd see them down in a ditch or upside down. I was afraid of getting stranded, conscious of what Rex would look like, frozen. The image of his little furry, ten-pound body as a monkey popsicle, if we were stranded for hours or days in the snow, kept me driving extra carefully.

At some point, the interstate was closed. State police and detour signs routed us off the highway onto an off-ramp, and it is no exaggeration to say that I slid into a hotel. My nerves were shot, and stranded motorists were everywhere. I booked Rex and I a room and unloaded our things before calling my husband who was on duty at the firehouse.

My near hysterical description of the stress and trauma of driving on a snow-obliterated interstate where there were no visible lines, passing multiple wrecks, and the heart-stopping, slip-sliding on ice and snow preceded my telling him, "Put plenty of money in the checking account because I'm not leaving here till spring."

He tried to talk me into trying to drive home the next day, but I was adamant about not getting on the highway again in the blizzard. Finally seeing that I wasn't budging, he said, "Okay, I'll be there in the morning to get you." He drove all night and woke Rex and I up around 5:00 a.m. Boy, we were one happy wife and monkey when he knocked on our door. Rex had easily picked up on my stress, and he chattered nonstop to Junior, wanting him to understand how bad it had been.

After he took a nap, he loaded us up. And since Rex was a smart monkey, he wouldn't let go of Junior's neck and rode back with his *daddy*. Junior told me to put my T-Bird's front-end five inches from his rear end and stay in his tire tracks. So I did, and we made it home all right. He always had my back. I guess I'll always feel the loss and the vulnerability that comes from not having him to call.

Again, I have been blessed by having someone who does check on me when I'm traveling, and he has promised to come to my aid if I am stranded or whatever. He has been a friend to our family for decades, and he promised Junior shortly before he died that he would watch out for me. Knowing my tendency for *adventure*, for lack of a better word, it was exceptionally kind for Steve Rainey to make that promise. He also happens to be my boss of twenty-five years (S.A.F.E. Planning) too, but he and his son, Blake, have gone out of their way to fulfill his voluntary obligation. Just to know there is somebody who is willing to have your back in times of trouble is comforting.

As the years go by, hopefully you develop a circle of family or friends you can call on but never with the assurance and ease of depending on your spouse. My husband's brother, sister, and their wife and husband came to my rescue more than once. After living in the apartment for six months, I bought a house that needed painting. But I broke a leg, so I wasn't able to do it. The four of them just showed up and worked two days getting the house ready for me to move into. The day I sold our motor home, it wouldn't start. Several people looked at it, and they all agreed that it must be dead batteries; but nobody could find the batteries. Junior's brother, Ricky, and his son, Cade, drove two hours to find and recharge the batteries. They were inside the steps in case this happens to anybody else. Four nephews from the Marze side, young men with families, gave me $100 bills to "help me out" at their uncle's funeral. I try to pay their generosity forward to new widows.

Chapter 3

DEPENDENCY

In thirty to sixty years together, to a certain extent, a man and woman become one unit, working together, building a life, a home, and raising a family together. Their personalities and individual roles evolve into a dependence upon each other, perhaps emotional, physical, and/or spiritual. When that unity is, using an apt Bible term, "torn asunder," the left behind half of the couple often feels like a fish on land, flopping around, trying to survive in a new world devoid of companionship, guidance, joy, strength, comfort, and even physical touch. A body torn asunder needs time to heal and rehabilitate. Some bodies heal faster than others. Some requires more professional rehabilitation. Others heal under their own power and pace.

I was asked to start a grief share group five years after I became a widow, and it was a mixed blessing in that hearing so many tragic stories of death and grieving was heartbreaking, but people receive comfort in sharing. The large number of people who are struggling to deal with widowhood can be depressing, yet the strength and courage demonstrated by these various personalities are also inspiring. It is sad though to see the ones who go years without coming to terms with their loss, shifting the burden of their care and contentment onto their children's shoulders or those of a friend because they are incapable of surviving alone. It's one thing for a couple to take oaths to share sickness and health, but when you make someone else responsible for your well-being and happiness, they are not always willing, and it can cause resentment and guilt.

The six hours between us restrict what my son and his family are able to do for me. But I know they are willing. And by their willingness, I have drawn strength and consolation, although my goal has been *not* to be dependent on my son and daughter. Having said that, I admit that I have and do depend on Phaedra and her family. They have been a rock for me. When I want company or help, they are there and willing, though I try not to burden them with my frequent presence or neediness.

I hear from widows all the time about how they couldn't survive without their sons and daughters and their families. I've also heard from sons and daughters about how their widowed mother's nonstop demands and complaints get on their nerves. When a woman loses her support system, she sometimes tries to find a replacement, which can be a burden on those she chooses.

Attention entrepreneurial: In a gathering of widows, someone typically mentions the need for a business specializing in *comfort* where widows can rent a man who will give hugs, share a meal, watch a movie with, or simply hold her hand—platonic demonstrations of caring and companionship that these women miss every day of their present reality. It seems like a little thing, but months and years of not having a man's arm around you or his hand to hold in times of stress, fear, and loneliness, the absence of touch is magnified over the years.

In the years since Junior was taken from me, it's hard not to have sad feelings, and maybe bitter ones, when your couple friends celebrate anniversaries. This is one of the sentiments you think will get better with time. But actually, it may be worse when years have passed. The first couple years after the funeral, you are in shock. Your mind has no way of imagining what it will be like later when it finally sinks in that the fiftieth bash your kids had planned for you or the anniversary cruise you'd both been looking forward to are never going to happen, at least not together. Some brave widows take an anniversary cruise alone, certainly not as satisfying as originally planned but does allow them to thumb their noses at fate.

I went on a cruise with a woman friend several months after widowhood. I appreciate Renee leaving her husband to come with me, and we had a good time, but that feeling of only being half there stayed with me. I do not know much about zombies, but what I've heard is how I felt like the walking dead, empty inside but moving forward, joyless but making an effort.

In these past years, I've had too many friends become widows due to COVID-19, cancer, and Alzheimer's. I don't sit at home brooding (often, anyway) but have tried to stay active and pay it forward by visiting and traveling with other widows because getting out of the house helps tremendously—a change of scenery and all that. It's a temporary balm; but when you navigate time in minutes and hours, just getting another day behind you is helpful.

*****

One thing a widow should learn is to become emotionally hardened during normal conversations at social gatherings. Until you have no husband, you probably haven't noticed how often wives show off (or share) special gifts from their sweet husbands or brag about trips and special events they are planning together. Wives are proud to show their new jewelry or cars or travel brochures, and you stand there with nothing to share because, for you, husbandly gifts are all in the past. It also occurs to you to wonder how many times in your pre-widowhood days you were blissfully unaware of husbandless women listening and hurting, reminders of happier times. *Widowhood* book readers have also told me this is true for divorced people.

Years pass, and sad spouses are left behind to mourn the lost dreams that are common to most marriages. They can't help but remember and regret the *what should have beens*. Twenty years down the widowhood road, some women are still speaking regretfully of the forsaken plans, like buying a lake house or living on a houseboat after retirement. That kind of thing just doesn't have the same appeal to a woman alone that it once did to a couple who dreamed of fun times together after retirement.

Retirement is something most of us look forward to. But in the best of marriages, there may be unexpected problems. There might be an adjustment period. Wives aren't always thrilled to have their husbands following them around all day, cooking him three meals a day, and losing their alone time. My particular retirement issue was that Junior immediately began to *help* me around the house. He rearranged the dishes in the kitchen cabinets, which meant that he put dishes up in the third shelf, which I leave empty because I was a foot shorter than him. I didn't want to have to climb a ladder to get dishes down. He forgot that he wasn't the captain at the fire station, bossing rookies around, and he would tell me "better" ways to make the beds, organize the pantry, and fold clothes.

I showed remarkable patience during those first weeks of adjustment; but finally, I had enough. The Bible says (Proverbs 21:9) that it is better for a man to live on the roof than to share a house with a quarrelsome wife. So when I have a problem with him, I try to *show* rather than *tell* (gripe and argue). While he was gone to Lowes one day, I went out to his man cave/workshop, and I reorganized his tools and rearranged his fishing lures by color.

When he came rushing into the kitchen that afternoon, telling me somebody had been messing in his shop, I gave him my sweetest smile and said, "That would be me. I wanted to reciprocate for all the help you've been giving me in the house." He got the message, and that was the end of that problem—what I wouldn't give to have those types of troubles again.

*****

Some of the well-meaning but irritating platitudes foisted off on new and hurting widows and widowers that wounded tender hearts still have the power to irritate us years later. We grow tired of hearing the same "*move on*" and "*find a new path for your life*" only because we think we have moved on and certainly believe we are walking a new path. Too many busybodies and concerned friends think that if a widow hasn't signed up for dating websites or are not partying every Saturday night that they aren't *moving on*. A little understanding might ease some of the heartache that is our burden to bear. Time heals, but each day is a battle to enjoy or tolerate the independence that a solitary life has forced upon us, ones left behind, wish the public was educated on what to say about their nonmarital status. If you want to minister to grieving people, look for a sensitive way to deal with their loss. Listen more. Talk less.

When I speak to groups, I share ways that friends and family can make grieving people feel better—not worse. I've been surprised at how many have told me that they made lists of the offensive remarks that people made to them. Not that people mean to say hurtful things; but unless we help them understand, they will keep doing it.

Then there are the ones who say enviously, "Boy, I can't wait till I have the house all to myself." Or "When my husband dies, I'm never cooking another meal." Oh, be careful what you wish for.

Some people never recover from a death of a spouse or child. Ten years after her husband died, an acquaintance remains severely depressed, and she's had professional counseling. She was even asked not to come back to her grief share group because she was "so negative." She knows that she was spoiled by her husband, and she can't get past the fact that nobody else in her life will do what he did for her. She, like others I've known, asks her friends and family to pray for her but refuses to help herself. She expects God to take all her pain away and maybe send a new Prince Charming to knock on her door. I explained to her that unless she has a thing for UPS drivers, that's probably not going to happen.

Bless our hearts! We have free will. God our Father supplies the strength we need, but He's not going to force us to get up from our tear-soaked pillows and gloomy, darkened rooms and keep on living to the best of our ability. To some people, this is a difficult concept. We should, of course, listen to their cries for help. But ultimately, each of us has to make the best of the life we have, even if it is not the life we chose.

Chapter 4

REMEMBERING

D on't be afraid to speak of the dearly departed. Give us permission to publicly share about those who have died in a world that often would rather we didn't talk about them. I understand. People are afraid we will cry. And we might, but that's all right. Tears can be cathartic, providing psychological relief.

Here's a truth for you: Nobody has the right to condemn you on how you repair your heart or how long you wallow in grief up to a point. Just as we have former relationships, past celebrations, and sorrows, your hurt is your own, and it will usually heal when it is time. Understanding by friends and families can help the healing process, but it cannot be forced.

No matter how many years pass, there are moments when you ache to bring your special someone down from heaven just to give them one more hug, hear their voice one more time, and to tell them how much you love and miss them.

After losing your special someone, you can be in a crowd of people but feel like you are totally alone. A few weeks after Junior died, I was sitting at a table with several people when a familiar, overwhelming urge came over me to hear Junior's voice, which was on our home answering machine. I dialed the number on my cell and listened to him tell me he would get back with me as soon as possible. I said, "I love you" before disconnecting, and one of the women at the table asked me who I'd called. Guess the "I love you" caught her attention.

"Junior," I answered. "I just wanted to hear his voice."

"Oh my Lord!" she exclaimed. "I didn't know you could do that, but if anybody could, I know you'd be the one!"

When I stopped laughing, I explained about the answering machine.

In modern society, we are inundated with political correctness on how to communicate with and about various races, religions, cultures, and sexual orientations; but grieving people have been left off the list.

It is my opinion and experience that sorrowful people have a short window of opportunity to whine and lament when people will listen with sympathy, but beyond that point, friends and family will begin avoiding you or criticizing you for being negative and boring. There are exceptions, such as other widows, but this is what happens in many cases; and it can and does cause hurt feelings.

There are perceptions that are relevant. When I was asked to join friends on a cruise, I heard one of the group complain about "little, old widow ladies" who had to have help carrying their bags and were a burden on the others. It brought to mind how, on our cruises, my late husband carried most of our luggage load, and once we hit ports, he claimed to be a pack mule for all my shopping "bargains." It occurred to me that I probably *would* need help, and that I would be the aforementioned little, old widow lady, a burden on others. I chose not to go.

A frequently mentioned heart pain among widows is that when they travel and reach their destination, there is no husband to call to tell, "I made it." When they leave their home, there is no concerned husband to hug them and tell them to drive safely, and the lack is felt.

I'm not normally a person who is comfortable with hugging and kissing people outside my immediate family, but when a friend was telling his wife goodbye because she was accompanying me on a road trip, I had a "widow's moment." They were hugging goodbye while I stood to the side watching, silently mourning the fact that I no longer have a husband to miss me or care about my safety. It was then that the husband looked up and motioned for me to come over to them. When I did, he put one arm around me and pulled me into the hug, including me in the goodbyes. Prewidowhood that might seem like a small thing, but that simple gesture touched me deeply. By sharing this incident, perhaps other people will realize what comfort a hug can be to a widow.

I'm sad to say that this man died from COVID-19, and now his wife is a sister widow with all the turmoil and loss that comes with it. RIP, Carter Sanders.

When you are married and you need physical comforting, you have the freedom to walk up to your husband, grab his arm, and pull it over your shoulder, snuggling up to him while soaking up his manly aura of strength and protection. He might be oblivious to your emotional distress if he's as insensitive as Junior was, but his nearness is still a comfort. Following widowhood, if you don't have a son, grandson, or close friend who are tuned in to your loss and needs and will hold you close every now and then, your life can be even colder and lonelier. When years pass, and, other than a handshake, you have not felt a man's touch, it causes something inside to shrivel up. I'm not really touchy-feely except for my grandkids, but it is a lack we all feel.

I've been criticized for calling my husband insensitive, but the fact was that if I had any emotional issues, I learned that I had to come out and tell him, "*You hurt my feelings*," or "*I'd really like to hit you right now*" because he wouldn't notice otherwise. It was a not-so-private joke between us. Instead of trying to change him, I learned to roll with it.

Dating again is a question I get asked a lot. A year after Junior died, I had a couple friend tell me that it was okay if I wanted to begin dating. I told them it had never occurred to me to seek their approval, especially due to the fact that if it were me dead and Junior left, he would have had a new woman on his way home from my funeral. That's a slight exaggeration but not by much. Not that he was a womanizer because he was all that was faithful and loyal, but I know how widowers are pursued by single women. Not all single women chase men, but enough of them do that it makes an impression.

Men have lots of stories about how single women are waiting for them when they come home from their wife's funeral with cakes and casseroles. One man told me his freezer was full of food from women just two weeks after his wife died, and they were still bringing "marriage bribes," he called them. One very nice man's old high-school girlfriend he hadn't seen in forty years came to his wife's funeral. They got married two weeks later.

Rumor has it that men are much more apt to remarry sooner than women. I have only gone out with a few men, and each one of them married within a short time of us dating. It's an odd feeling, dating after forty and fifty years of being married. Instead of your parents meeting your "boyfriend," now your date has to pass muster with your adult kids and grandkids. Leaving to go to the movie one night, my man friend asked one of my granddaughters what time he should bring me home. "Eight o'clock," she said. "But it's seven o'clock now," he protested. "Eight o'clock," she insisted. I didn't make curfew that evening. I stayed out late, till around 10:00 p.m.

Whereas some of my widow friends jumped right into kissing and hugging, some of us haven't felt that easy about the physical side of mature dating. That's all I've got to say about it, but that's probably why I'm still single.

*****

No amount of anxiety can change the future. No amount of guilt can change the past. I advise my married friends who nitpick one another to beware life's delicacy. Circumstances can change suddenly. The widows I've met, who are overcome with guilt, have a difficult time finding peace. If the last words you say are ones of anger, spoken with meanness, you will have a lot of time to regret it.

It sounds silly, but I feel guilty because when I cooked cabbage and onions for Junior, he wanted me to cut the cabbage in itty-bitty strips. It wouldn't have taken that much longer, but I cut larger pieces because it was faster and easier. Such a silly thing, but it comes to mind now and then regrets and guilt that I didn't do it the way I knew he liked it best. Uncomfortable memories come to mind. He would have laughed. I'm just so thankful that no harsh words had been spoken between us when he died. That would have been hard to live with.

Some people bounce back easier than others. When my mother's boyfriend of eight years died, men asked her for a date before we left the funeral, which was on a Saturday morning. Later that day, Don's ashes sat on her kitchen table as we discussed the ceremony when she got a call from another man wanting to cheer her up by taking her out the next day. Her response was, "Well, since we just memorialized Don today, I hate to start dating so soon as tomorrow, but what about Monday?"

At my incredulous look, she said, "Well, Elaine, at my age, we can't afford to wait around too long."

Chapter 5

HELP!

I t is nice when men friends and family members pack their tool kits when visiting a single woman because we've always got a screw that needs tightening, a bulb that needs swapping out, or something that needs to be nailed up. In my Louisiana house, the only plug in the front yard for the leaf blower or Weedwacker was in the porch roof. Now how smart was that? When you are five feet tall, you can't reach ceilings without climbing up a ladder. I broke my leg a few months after my husband died, and that left me absolutely paranoid about climbing. I won't do it because I do *not* want to break another leg. I fell all over the place on crutches! I had to have help getting on the potty and to get a bath! It was a horrible experience made worse by not having my husband to hold me up and wait on me. Years before I was on crutches, when our first grandchild was born, and it wasn't nearly as catastrophic because I had *him*. It made a huge difference not having him for this last broken bone.

Men, check on your single women acquaintances because many of us haven't been conditioned to think about oil stickers, tires, air-conditioning filters, and fireplace dampers. It takes a while to learn to do all that stuff. My attic flooded because I didn't know to check the pan on an attic water heater. Though whoever decided it was a good thing to put a water heater in the attic was not thinking smart—my opinion.

Prewidowhood, there are ways to make life easier, though some people cannot contemplate thinking about it. It takes looking ahead. If you won't be able to afford to hire everything done that your husband used to do, I suggest you learn how to do yard work and house repairs. Learn where the electrical box is and all about the fuses and hope they are where you can reach them. After Junior died, the electricity went out, and I finally found the fuse box eight feet off the floor in the garage. Thank God for tall friends who can climb ladders. Living up in the mountains, we had propane. And one time, I let the tank go dry. I called the gas company for a refill, but I spent a few days without gas.

If your husband has a firewood guy or a chimney cleaner that he uses, get their phone numbers. Find out who he trusts to help you take care of your car. I had three flats after my husband died in the first two months. I didn't know how to change a tire; I couldn't even find the spare tire. It was like life conspired to make me think I could not make it alone. I bought a car in Louisiana, drove it back to Arkansas, and didn't bother to register it because nobody told me too. I thought all the paperwork we did at the car dealership took care of all that. A man friend finally noticed my temporary license plate was out of date and told me I had to register the car and pay Arkansas taxes. There's a fine for waiting too long. Who knew?

It's a good advice *if* your husband has a long illness. Of course, with a sudden death, it will not work. Try to get him to give away any tools or men toys to people predeath, or have him make lists of who he wants to get what. I had engraved name tags made with our kids and grandkids names, and my husband labeled which guns went to whom. I learned quickly that most buyers weren't going to give me blue book value for trailers, tractor, and such. I've heard men say that they love to get to widows soon after their husbands die because they can get good deals on all his "stuff." Some widows have told me they auctioned their husband's equipment off but didn't feel like they got full value. Like when I sold one of my husband's metal trailers for

$1500, the buyer told me, "It's worth a whole lot more." I waited for him to give me a whole lot more; it didn't happen.

I wish I could have kept our motor home, but I couldn't drive it without taking down mailboxes. And after dealing with a backed-up sewage tank, I was ready to sell it. I loved that fine motor home, but I couldn't handle it alone.

Have your spouse (and yourself) write letters to family members. Or make videos to leave them. To read or watch a communication from one who has departed this life is so sustaining, especially during the first months and years. Memories are great, but to have a message assuring you of that special love and connection—well, it is a healing balm to a hurting heart. Junior wrote letters to me, his mother, our kids, and grandkids. When the loneliness gets to me, I read my letters, and it is like he is close by. Some say they can't read his letters because it makes them too sad, but it also keeps his memory alive. Nobody wants to be forgotten.

Some women cannot or will not stay alone. Some go from family members to friends and do not stay in their own home for the first six months or longer. They travel from house to house rather than face a night alone in their home surrounded by memories that will never be again. Martha swore she only went in her house during the daytime for a full year after her husband died. Then there are the ones whose spouse died in their home, in their bed, who cannot force themselves to ever sleep there again.

Go out to eat because meals alone can be depressing. Develop a group of friends who will keep you company. Prior to COVID, a group of widows and I went out to eat lunch nearly every day. Lunch prices are cheaper than dinners, plus you can take leftovers home so you don't have to cook that night.

Help yourself by actively trying not to wallow in your misery. When holidays and anniversaries are coming up, make a plan. Leave or invite company over. Don't be alone. On the anniversary of Junior's death, my daughter and her kids go with me to the VA hospital to deliver books, and then we go to a nearby bakery that Junior loved to go to. We deliberately bring up special memories that usually bring tears but smiles also.

It always comes back to this fact, your life is irrevocably changed. Most of us do not like the change, did not ask for the change, and we want to live in that former time to savor memories of that better time. It's not easy to face an unknown future. But if we are left here, we must keep living by the grace we have been given. We must be willing to roll with our new reality and make the best of a complicated, challenging situation.

Good intentions count, but I read something that I could not help but relate to: *I don't feel like I'm terribly important to anyone anymore. I just kinda exist in people's lives.*

And just as laughter adds to a marriage, after a death, it may be a long time before you find your joy again. But find it. You must if you intend on being the best widow you can be. It takes time, such as the story I will end this book with since it is a good example of how it takes time before you can laugh about certain incidents.

I've never sued anybody in my life, but I seriously considered suing the company responsible for a hot wax hair removal kit I bought. I told Junior I was going to sue them, and he laughed so hard, saying he would love to be in court for *that* testimony that I decided not to pursue it. It was so traumatizing that it took a solid year before I could write about it, only to warn other women so they will not go through the same thing. It is now apparent I'm not the only one who has had a bad experience with this product. A recent email about a woman who was stuck to her bathtub for hours, and friends who have confessed similar humiliating experiences, has convinced me there is a need for an "outing" on hot wax hair removal kits!

A lot of women in the over-fifty age bracket are not experienced in the hot wax method of hair removal. An old-fashioned razor usually does the trick for us, but as I was browsing in the hygiene products one day, I found a hot wax kit designed to use at home. It guaranteed unwanted body hair would be nonexistent for up to six weeks. That sounded good because my husband and I were leaving for a cruise in the coming weeks, and I thought, how nice it would be not to shave my legs for the duration.

The directions were simple: melt the wax in a microwave, use the waxing stick to spread the wax, let it harden, and rip the unwanted hair off. It did say to do a six-inch strip at a time and to start at the ankle and work up. But the directions *should* have emphasized the reason for this method. I am a busy woman, so I usually try the fast track of doing things. *If* the directions had been more explicit about the dangers of waxing, I would have been forewarned about potential problems.

I am going to be very delicate here in my word description for obvious reasons, but imagine you are naked (you are supposed to shower first to moisturize your skin before applying the hot wax). Instead of beginning at my ankle and working up, I decided to begin with my thigh since this was the biggest and closest spot to work on. It seemed logical to practice the spreading technique on the most accessible part before I worked my way down to areas harder to reach. After all, my body does not bend as easily as it used to. After covering my thighs with an extra thick layer of hot wax *first*, following the theory that if a little is good, a lot should be better, I bent over and began spreading it upward from my ankle, planning to merge the wax at my knee. Be advised that the wax cools and hardens rather quickly.

This is the part where the telling gets delicate. You may have to actually do this to fully understand what happened. While I was bent over, waxing my lower leg, a certain other area was touching my hot waxed thighs. In hindsight, it should have occurred to me that anything that touched the wax would stick, but at the time, I was concentrating on the application of the hot dripping wax. As the wax hardened, a certain "private" part of my anatomy became stuck to my thighs—Super Glue stuck! Still unaware of the problem, I finished waxing the lower part of my leg while in the bending over stance, which put top body parts on lower parts. All the time I was thinking how smart I was to dehair a whole leg at one time instead of the six-inch strips recommended in the instructions. I was going to get this done in record time.

But when I tried to stand upright, I could not because my bosoms were stuck to other parts of me! Now I do not cry easily, but the next few hours of trying to get unstuck nearly brought me to hysterics. I kept remembering news reports of people who called 911 after getting their head stuck in something stupid or the woman who got a tire swing stuck around her chest. The image of emergency medical teams trying to remove my "private" self from other private body parts while the local news filmed the event gave me the incentive to basically mutilate myself trying to get loose.

After the initial shock of being stuck in a bent-over position began to sink in, the pain of trying to remove my body parts from each other while in that awkward position began. The hardened wax was having an intense reaction to every action I took. I cut with scissors until they were too gunky to work. Then I covered the involved parts with ice, intending to freeze the wax and break it off. It worked to some small degree. I tried scraping with a knife, spoon, and anything else I could get my hands on. I got in a bathtub of nearly scalding water. All that did was melt enough of the wax that it ran into creases it should not have gone into. (This is where I related to a friend who became stuck to the bathtub.)

This is powerful wax! Next, I used baby oil, cooking oil, and olive oil, thinking the oil would cause the wax to slide off. It only made the scissors harder to hold while I was trying to free body hair in low places from the wax. One problem was that there was not much room to maneuver, bent over as I was. I ended up cutting skin along with the hair/wax combination. But even then, the pain was not equal to the humiliation.

And, yes, knowing that the whole point of hair removal by waxing is to rip it away, I did try that. Ever read about the torture technique of ripping fingernails off? Well, I promise you, this is similar! After two hours of desperately trying everything known to cut, rip, or melt hair and wax, I was finally able to stand upright, though I was hurting from all the places skin was missing. Parts not still covered by wax or scalded were bleeding. Exhausted and in tears, I put on a cotton robe (forget underwear) and sat down just as my husband came home. His usual attentive self, after thirty-five years of marriage, didn't notice anything was wrong until I tried to stand up and my robe was stuck to everything below my waist from all the wax residue, including the chair.

Plus, and again, I'm trying to be delicate here, the near-scalding water caused some of the wax to melt and run into any crevice, crack, or wrinkle, and I have several. Those areas were sticking to each other and anything else with which they came into contact.

While I was trying to explain my dilemma, my husband demonstrated why I sarcastically refer to him as Mr. Sensitivity. Due to his laughing during my time of anguish, it was probably a good thing I was stuck to the chair! By the way, wax soaks through cotton, and cotton sticks to leather. That was when I was threatening to sue the hair removal kit company.

After I managed to get unstuck from the chair, I couldn't remove the robe (without ripping away more skin), except by cutting it free. My husband had to do the hardest-to-reach places during the few times he could stop laughing long enough to use his knife to cut. All the scissors had to be thrown away because they were so gummed up that they would never be any good again. I was left with pieces of fabric stuck to various wax globs still attached to my body. Mr. Sensitivity kept mentioning a resemblance to a plucked chicken, and I was homebound for days because my clothes stuck to me. Eventually, with numerous hot showers and continual ice treatments to freeze and break off chunks of wax and the loss of the skin it was attached to, I was able to dress. Thankfully, all the Band-Aids and gauze patches did not show.

So, ladies, *if* you are ever so foolish to decide to do hot wax hair removal, just take it from me and *don't*. Go to a professional or stick to shaving your legs because if four of us, that I know of, had similar experiences, there's no telling how many other women have too. There are definitely more out there. The embarrassment just keeps them from telling!

Ten Years Gone

When we hear the word *anniversary*, most people think about a joyful celebration, but for unfortunate others, it can mean an acknowledgment of a death. Ten years ago today, my husband left his cancer-ridden body as he also left me, his son, his daughter, five grandchildren, his mother, his mother-in-law, three brothers, a sister, and numerous other family and friends to mourn and miss him. And we have done so with a vengeance.

It's been ten years since their daddy was there to help build things with and for Daniel and Phaedra or put his arms around them and share their joy or troubles or to give them advice on finances or work. It's been ten years since he'd taken the grandkids fishing or four-wheeler riding. Sadly, he didn't get to watch them get older or Kinsley crowned homecoming queen and graduate high school or Hagen and Garrison win shooting competitions. He missed Colton and Makenna's basketball games and teaching them to drive. So many "should haves!" So many missed opportunities to be the absolute best dad and papa he was born to be.

Ten years ago, I lost the man who had given me his strength through hurts and sadness. He'd been my comfort and protector, my best friend, the open arms I ran to, and the wide chest I rested on. Unlike some couples, we were totally united in our politics, religion, morality, beliefs in our constitutional rights, child rearing, humor, and enjoyment of our marriage of thirty-nine and a half years. The loss was profound, indescribable.

How many lonely nights and meals are there in ten years? How many missed occasions, special events, and lost opportunities with the kids? Men and women were not made to be alone, I think. But some of us, through no fault of our own, have lost the opportunity and blessing to grow old with our life-mate and instead had to face the future alone without the physical presence and support system of the one we desired and loved—a huge "should have been."

Forgive me for being melancholic on this tenth anniversary of Junior's death. Please don't give me sympathy or advice. I've had plenty of both. I know all the scriptures. My faith is firm, but my emotions are not always on that higher plain.

In summary: "Lord, once upon a time you gave me a rare man, and I loved him well…as he did me."

Papa holds his newborn grandson three months before
he dies. He can only talk with a mechanical device
but five year old Hagen Marze doesn't mind.

Colton and Hagen entertain their Papa with funny stories.

Knowing he was terminal, we spent as much time together with the family as possible. Papa helps Makenna pet a dolphin.

Our mothers pose with us at Stephenie and Daniel's wedding.

I was a 19 year old college student, and he was 23, straight
out of the Navy after two tours in Vietnam.

Enjoying our four grandbabies!

This young firefighter loved "fighting fires and saving lives."

Kinsley loved hiking and wading with her Papa.

Junior and the kids surprised me with a family portrait for my birthday.

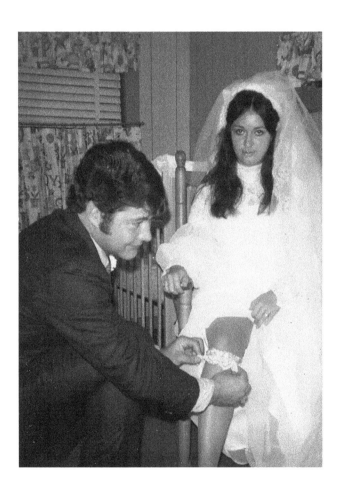

Phaedra lived nearby, but Daniel had a six hour drive to come visit his dad. This photo was taken two months before death.

Our thirty-second wedding anniversary. We had
no idea we would not make the 40th.

About the Author

Elaine Hodge Marze is a former newspaper and magazine editor, writer, and publisher from Louisiana who presently lives in Northwest Arkansas. She combines her factual reporting style with humor in this book and Hello, Darling, a book of faith about the heroic battle with cancer fought by her husband and family. Readers say they've never read books on dying and cancer that were humorous before.

.